# Growing Mentor Intelligence™
# A Field Guide To Mentoring

## Alan D. Landry

An ALtuitive Holdings, LLC Publication
with Deuxology Publishing

ISBN: 978-0-9911612-1-8

Printed in the U.S.A.

First Print Edition

# Growing Mentor Intelligence™
# A Field Guide to Mentoring

## Alan D. Landry

An ALtuitive Holdings, LLC Publication
with Deuxology Publishing

This book is dedicated to my wife,
Paula,
for teaching me commitment,
believing in me,
and
giving me hope
that I could change the world
for the better.

6

# CONTENTS

# Acknowledgements

This book has been a labor of love. It gives voice to the incredible impact of mentorship in my life and to all those who saw more in me than I did in myself. These mentors grew me, created opportunity for me, and above all, invested themselves in me. They taught me what right looks like, and this book is about learning how to give that back to others. It is a "how to" guide, an acknowledgement that mentorship involves skills that can be learned and taught, positively changing the lives of both mentors and those who are mentored in the process. It is about growing your own Mentor Intelligence™.

Among the many wonderful mentors that I have had over the years, I want to give special thanks to Betsy Holden, Tom Tuohy, Chuck Wood, Russ Moore, Don Ingram, Mike Thornton, Chuck Smith and Jim Riley for teaching me the importance of mentorship. I also want to acknowledge the special role two Army chaplains, Jim Watson and Tim Bedsole, have played in my life. To you and to the dozens of other unnamed men and women who invested in me, know that your mentorship has lasted a lifetime, and continues to find life in the hearts and souls of my mentees today.

For all my former and current mentees, thanks for giving a more noble meaning to my life, for giving me something to believe in and something to give back. Thank you for teaching me what significance is all about.

Finally, I want to thank my family for their continued love and support, to everyone who took the time to review and comment on my drafts, and especially to Dr. Amanda Goodson and Tom Tuohy for motivating me to put these words to paper.

# Forward

I consider being asked to write the forward of Colonel Alan Landry's book to be one of the greatest honors of my life. Col. Landry personifies leadership and he is the living example of mentorship. Col. Landry has been battle tested with life experiences and the accomplishments of a very few. Yet he possesses the humility and honor of even fewer. This book and its chronicles are a testament to the man and they are a roadmap for each of us. Reading this book will remind you that we are all called upon to be leaders. Each of us needs mentors and we each have the responsibility to be a mentor. None of us has gotten to our place in life alone and we stand little chance of reaching the future we envision without the guidance of mentors.

There is a longing in every person to live the life they imagine. Along the way we face challenges and heartbreak we can never anticipate. In many respects our lives are a suspension between random moments. How can we navigate those moments? How can we stay the course, or explore a new path that destiny has delivered to us? We can only do so with the help of others. Col. Landry's chronicles provide you with the outline to find those you need and, most importantly, to be that person for others.

Albert Pine wrote, "What we do for ourselves dies with us. What we do for others and the world remains and is immortal." The best way to find a mentor is to be one. Our time on this earth is measured by our contributions. When we open ourselves to giving and build our lives on a foundation of generosity, the gifts we give are returned to us tenfold. When you seek to mentor, the mentors you require will show up on your path. These chronicles can be the outline of your strategy

11

of living a generous life. In return, they will guide you in being able to accept that generosity in your time of need.

This isn't a book that teaches you how to get ahead in life. This book is a reminder that you only succeed when we all succeed. It is a book for everyone because it is written by a man and a leader who embraces everyone. Col. Landry has experienced war, yet he knows the only victory is peace. He has worked in the highest levels of business, yet he understands success is in people, not profits. He looks at every person and only sees their humanity. As with every great mentor and extraordinary leader Col Landry has the vision to see past age, gender, race, religion, disability and sexual orientation and embrace the true essence of another fellow human being.

On these pages you are given a gift from an author with a 20/20 vision of humanity. Col Landry provides you with clarity and the strategy to give and receive as the leader you were born to be. I encourage you to read this book slowly, keep it close, refer to it often and apply its principles in your work, your family, and in your expanded network. You will be reminded to always lead from your heart and you will be forever blessed with a blueprint for living a life of great value.

Tom Tuohy is the founder of Dreams for Kids, Inc, CEO, Dreams for Kids Foundation, CEO, Dream Leaders University and author of *Dreams for Kids, Changing the World...One Person at a Time.*

# Preface

In spite of all our technological advances, today we live in a world that has created the greatest isolation and "at-risk" population than ever before. Across the generations we all seek understanding, acceptance, guidance, support and advocacy as we face our own unique challenges and seek the meaning in our lives. The core topic of this book - effective mentorship or what I call Mentor Intelligence™ - is a simple and effective answer to that need. Yet just as the need seems greatest, the practice of mentorship seems wanting, whether in the work place, in our schools, our organizations, or any other place where we gather as people.

This book was written to address that gap. By enhancing our ability to mentor others as well as to be more effectively mentored by others, it can change our lives for the better. It can also change our world, how we relate to it, and how to increase our own sense of self-worth. We need to change the conversation about the topic, turn some traditional ideas upside down, and replace them with different perspectives that offer empowerment for anyone willing to invest the time and energy regardless of circumstance, organization or experience.

So who is this book for? In a sense, it is written for anyone who has ever mentored anyone as well as for anyone who has ever wanted to be mentored. To those of you who are already mentors, I hope that you find something of value in these pages that will make you better mentors. For those of you hoping that someone will just say "yes" to mentoring you, create the future that you want to be. Within these pages are techniques and tools that can help you learn how to navigate life's challenges while discovering how to give that gift back to others. Learn what Mentor Intelligence™ is all about, and more importantly, how to grow your own. Empowerment is at your fingertips if you are willing to put the effort into it.

The pages that follow will introduce you to mentorship as a way of being rather than just a good thing to do. I will offer you unique perspectives on mentoring, provide practical tools to help you increase your proficiency as a mentor partner, and offer you a process that will allow you to help create life strategies, both for yourself and for others. Each chapter presents a different aspect about mentorship and offers both perspectives and tools to help each of us grow on our own personal journeys. At the end of each chapter, I have included a short summary of key points called *"A Blueprint For Exploring Possibilities."* Because this is a practical guide, I have also created a separate page at the end of each chapter providing *"Questions for Personal Reflection and Growth."* Besides the almost magical connection between writing down our thoughts and perspectives and opening our hearts and minds, there is also something powerful and liberating about putting our thoughts and feelings into words. I encourage you to create a mentorship journal, if you have not already done so, and watch the growth as your effort and commitment are rewarded.

Above all, for each of you reading this book, know that you have the power to change a life, one person at a time, to turn adversity into advantage, to offer a hand up rather than a hand out, to teach life skills that will live far beyond your life, and to create opportunity for others where today there is none. This is the essence of leadership, it is the essence of good mentorship, and it is the core of leading a life of significance rather than a life of self-importance. Take a chance, step out of your comfort zone, reach out to someone and become a mentor, and be changed for the better in the process. There is no greater gift than to create purposeful change in another person's life, giving back all that you have been given in your own life.

# Chapter One: Fulfilling Your Greatest Need

## *Why Are You Here?*

So why is this book necessary? Isn't our greatest need to be accepted for the unique whole person that we are, and to bring that whole person to every aspect of our life? Yet everywhere I turn, the same questions (among many others) come up time and again indicating that this greatest need is often unfulfilled:

- Why am I here? What is my unique purpose in life and how do I align what I do in the work place to that purpose?
- How can I be true to myself and to my values in the workplace? What does it mean to be authentic?
- What should my short and long-term life goals be? How can I achieve them?
- How can I balance my home life and my work life?
- How can I navigate the social and political waters at work or in my organization?
- What is my best career path and how should I choose among various options?

- How can I increase my network so more people know about the work that I do?
- How do I deal with a difficult boss or difficult teammate?

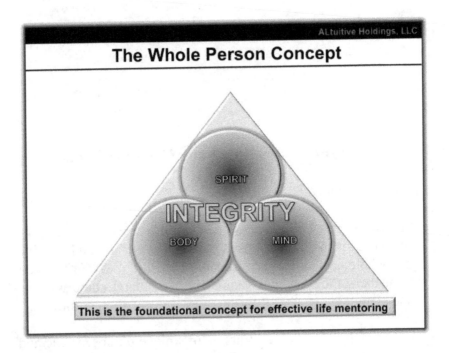

Figure 1.0 The Whole Person Concept

Our first step on this journey is the whole person concept I first learned about when I was a student at the United States Military Academy at West Point, New York. Each of us is a very unique and special creation; unique in mind, unique in body, and unique in spirit. This frames the concept of integrity better than anything else I have ever seen as wholeness in mind, body and spirit. Wholeness demands that the person each of us brings to work is the same person we bring home to our families and friends, and vice versa.

Perhaps this concept is not new to you. As with many things in life, sometime those that are the most obvious to see are the most difficult to put into practice. I have observed the consequences of trying to be a different person at work than at home. I view this as highly unnatural. To fracture yourself to "fit in" or to "be accepted" means that you must be less than your full self at work. Not only is this a waste of human potential, it will ultimately fail as you compromise in both home life and work life to be someone you are not.

The whole person concept is a foundational principal of my mentorship philosophy. It is why my approach is both effective and life changing because it aims at the heart of the matter – learning how to be whole.

We have become a society that focuses more on information rather than on relationships, on gratification rather than discipline, on self-importance rather than significance, and on entitlement and status rather than responsibility. Ironically, information in all its forms and shapes (perhaps it is data rather than information) is more available today than ever before, but it is overwhelming and detached, void of the very human and empowering characteristics that we all need today. Many of our children regardless of social or economic status are living in an emotional, mental and spiritual vacuum, awash in information but void of meaningful relationships. They want to be whole to themselves but need help along the way. That is what mentorship is all about.

There is something about the human condition that seems to drive a need to belong, to feel appreciated and valued, and to grow and be developed beyond what we are today in every person at every level. The need is not isolated to our youth or to early career employees. It is about each of us, the connections that link us to one another and give our lives deep meaning, and the opportunities that we have to grow as we share our unique journeys. Good mentorship is the glue that ties us to one another, across the generations and across possibilities that we are not able to see alone. It is also the most powerful solution to the isolation that affects us at work, at school, at home, and everywhere else we go, because in the end, it is about investing in meaningful relationship that provides mutual benefit to both mentee and mentor.

### The Workplace Connection

As the need to belong, to connect and to grow is increasing in both our personal and work lives and the need for mentorship is expanding, my experience has been too few organizations have effective, meaningful programs. Frequently, key leaders are not willing to take on the role of mentor, and where organizational mentor programs do exist, they can lack the authenticity and senior leader support so critical to success. My challenge to the leaders of companies who do have organic programs is to survey your early career employees anonymously and authentically and get their honest opinion where there is no chance for retribution. If you ask them, they will tell you the truth, if they think you really want to know. If you don't like what you hear, listen to their voices, read on, and lead the change that needs to happen.

Mentoring is one of those programs that can easily fall through the cracks. Human Resource (HR) departments usually acknowledge the need but often lack the resources or senior leader support to develop comprehensive, effective programs. Some organizations create mentor programs, but absent the soul and the spirit of what true mentorship needs to provide, they do not work. It can be a great sound bite as companies market themselves as employers of choice, but when the reality fails to match the promise, the result is disappointment, frustration and disillusionment.

The real challenge is that no one seems to "own it" – mentoring is, after all, deeply personal and is therefore a personal choice, right? Perhaps the more important question is "Should it be optional?" I believe that mentorship is a basic requirement of good leadership and that it is therefore an obligation of every leader in every organization. No one should be excused because it's hard or simply because they do not want to do it. To do so is to abrogate a leader's responsibility to grow the next generation.

Mentorship is a discipline that requires the application of skills that can be taught and learned, and that is the real reason for this book. When I look across my network, especially at the 20-30 year olds, they reflect both the hunger for meaningful mentorship, and the void as well. It does not have to be this way. What if mentorship were defined by senior leadership of every organization as a basic part of the organization's culture? What if mentorship was something valued from the top down and encouraged at every level? What would that mean in the workplace and how can we make this possibility real? As with most pressing problems in life, it seems there are three possible responses: do nothing, do the wrong thing, or figure out the right thing to do. This book is offered as a blueprint for exploring constructive possibilities and developing Mentor Intelligence™. I don't claim to have all the right answers (no one does), but I do offer practical tools that any person can master, and change themselves and others in the process.

## *A Blueprint for Exploring Possibilities*

(1) Each of us is a unique creation of mind, body and spirit with unique purpose, opportunity and needs – this is the whole person concept. Our greatest need as individuals is

to be able to bring our whole self to every aspect of our life. This whole person concept defines integrity and provides the critical context for personal mentorship. It is also the key to understanding the more difficult questions in any person's life.

(2) We are more isolated today than ever before across every social and economic class. This is especially significant among our youth and early career employees. Isolation limits personal growth and limits our human potential at home, at work and every other place we interact. Mentorship is a powerful antidote to that isolation and can become the key to finding your whole self or helping someone else find theirs.

(3) Mentorship is a basic leader responsibility and a discipline – even a way of life – that can be taught and learned. It can become the glue that ties our unique journeys together in meaningful ways to create a future of growth and possibility. It is a game changer for a better world.

*Chapter One Practical Exercise*
*Questions For Personal Reflection and Growth*

1. Have you ever been exposed to the "whole person" concept? How does it make you feel? Have you ever been in a home, school or work situation where you felt that you could not be yourself? Describe how that made you feel. How did you deal with it?

2. Have you ever felt isolated at home or at work? What caused the isolation? How did you handle it? Did anyone reach out to you and help you through the situation? How did they do it? What worked best and what did not work at all?

3. Have you ever had a mentor in your life? What did that person do to help you? What did they ask of you and what did you ask of them? How did you thank them?

4. Has someone whom you asked to serve as a mentor for you ever turned you down? Did they tell you why? What did you do about it?

5. Have you ever been asked to be a mentor? How did you answer? Do you believe that you have the right skills to be a good mentor? Can these skills be learned? Are you willing to try?

# Chapter Two:  What is Mentoring?

*Creating A Baseline – What Really Matters*

Once I was asked to give a presentation on mentorship to a women's organization.  Based on a number of conversations I had before the presentation, it seemed that a lot of confusion surrounded the definition, depending upon individual experiences.  To create a baseline for the group, I acknowledged that while the precise definition might be elusive, it is also irrelevant.  The important common pieces that can be extracted from most of the traditional definitions are that (1) mentoring is a process that is centered on investing in a relationship that evolves over time, (2) it focuses on personal development, and (3) it provides the mentee with access, support and knowledge they otherwise could not get.

In this admittedly conventional view, the more senior mentor "gifts" the junior mentee with the benefit of experiences, lessons learned, observations, possibilities, and access to a network otherwise not available.  What is less appreciated is that in this process, the mentor is changed as well, benefitting from a concept called reverse mentorship wherein the mentee "gifts" the mentor with insights, perspectives, experiences and a network not otherwise available to the mentor.

## Toward A More Progressive Future

But what about the countless people who do not live in that conventional world or work in hierarchical organizations? While most of my experience has been in the conventional type of mentorship, I believe that more egalitarian forms of mentorship replacing the terms mentor and mentee with "mentor partners" are not only possible, but perhaps more relevant today than other forms. This is especially true for the generations of young adults who are looking to change the conversation around mentorship while still creating meaningful, effective mentor relationships. Such mentoring is based on mutually beneficial relationship of <u>equal</u> partners, taking the terms "junior" and "senior" completely out of the equation. Each partner brings his or her unique value to the relationship without regard to positional power, yet it is still about challenging each other with insights, perspectives, lessons learned, and networks. This type of mentorship is not as radical as it seems, because at its core is the same mutual respect, investment and "gifting" that defines the best traditional mentor relationships.

Whatever your definition of mentorship, traditional or progressive, the tools, techniques and procedures of Growing Mentor Intelligence™ have universal application and will not only improve the effectiveness of the mutual relationship, but also empower anyone who uses them to gain control over their options, their decisions and ultimately over their lives. The old adage "The more you give, the more you get" is most certainly true when it comes to mentorship regardless of style or circumstance.

## Personal "Mentoring" Styles That Do Not Work

At this point it might be useful to reflect on what mentoring should not be. As you read this section, if you find yourself wondering how true these perspectives are, talk it over with your mentees to gain their perspectives. They should get the deciding vote on what works and what does not!

The most unsuccessful mentoring approach that I have observed occurs when a well-intentioned mentor feels obligated to "fix" something about the mentee. Most people, understandably so, resent someone trying to do this to them. A number of mentees whom I have talked with over the years describe this as one of the more painful "failure" modes. It typically plays out like this: the mentor is a successful executive who believes that he or she has the best solution to whatever problem the mentee is facing. Intending to help the mentee, they drive the mentee to "fix" or "correct" whatever it is about them that "gets in the way." Rather than exploring options and finding one that best fits the mentee's whole self, the focus of the mentoring is on what the mentor would do in the same situation. Trying to "fix" someone is not only detrimental, it is doomed to fail and will likely fracture the relationship in the process. What works for one person is not likely to fit exactly the same way that it does for another person. More importantly, the mentor does not have to live with the consequences of the decision, no matter how well intentioned. Even if a mentee asks for your recommendation on how to deal with a certain situation, I encourage you to be very cautious, focusing more on options and consequences and allowing the mentee to remain in the driver's seat.

There is a related and more dangerous style where mentors try to "recreate" their mentees in their image and likeness rather than accepting the qualities and gifts of the mentee at face value as unique and whole. This is a direct assault on the whole person concept for the mentee. Such an egocentric mentor is likely to focus their energy only on those who are most like them to the exclusion of everyone else. This is the opposite of diversity and inclusion and can severely limit development, growth and opportunity to a single personality style, culture, social status, or worse, race or ethnic persuasion. It is a very subtle form of discrimination that I have seen play out at some very high organizational levels. Sameness in mentoring is likely to breed sameness in opportunity guised under the mask of "chemistry." I will have a lot more to say about chemistry later. For now, my core message is for all leaders to be open to mentoring others regardless of how different or close they seem to the mentor's personal style or personality.

## *"Form Over Substance"*

Failure modes can also apply to mentor programs as well as to individual mentoring. While it's clear that organizations which lack mentor programs are not likely to create a sustained culture of mentorship, there is actually something worse – organizations that create formal mentor programs missing the "heart and soul" of what mentorship is all about.

Such programs most often place format and appearance over substance, and in the process, establish negative precedence and give mentorship a bad name. This can occur when: (1) senior leaders direct the addition of mentor quotas on performance development goals without providing the tools or training to make the goal real or achievable for mentors or mentees, or (2) the organization establishes programs but assigns them for action to employees who lack the experience to successfully create and execute an effective program. Quotas are likely to drive "check-the-box" leader behaviors at the expense of the program and the mentees. In the latter case, some well-meaning manager may work tirelessly to create an effective program, but if the senior organizational leaders opt out, the program will not succeed.

A quick scan of the number of senior level mentor participants and the number of mentees each senior leader accepts can establish a meaningful answer to the form over substance question. A mentor program worth its salt with heart and soul will be widespread across the organization, and every senior organizational leader will be engaged purposefully and gladly to the benefit of all.

### The Risk of Elite Programs

Perhaps more controversial is my contention that exclusive mentor programs involving relatively small groups of junior leaders also miss the mark. These programs typically focus just on a very select group of promising young employees who spend one or two years immersed in the business. They receive the very best of everything - access, leader development and mentoring. These leaders are often selected before they have spent any significant time in the work place proving their promise, but their selection identifies them as special among their peers.

While these programs do a lot of good for selected participants, they leave the rest out of the mix to fend for themselves. The selected participants may begin to view themselves as more deserving, or better than those not selected, fostering an elitism that can prove corrosive to organizational cohesion, as well as to basic leader development.

Creating haves and have-nots is the opposite of diversity and inclusion and it is the antithesis of what any good mentor program should create. Solid mentor programs are inclusive rather than exclusive, egalitarian rather than elitist, and they serve to grow an entire organization rather than a select slice. Doesn't everyone deserve to be mentored and developed? Who would you deny that to?

*Ambition, Promotions and Challenging Bosses*

As I close out this chapter, I wanted to add two final thoughts. Generalizations are seldom productive, so I will avoid making one here. What I will say is that a lot of the early career employees I know and have worked with are highly ambitious – they want to get promoted. This is not a bad thing in itself, but if self-promotion is the underpinning of a request for a mentor, that agenda will be transparent and it is not the basis for building a strong mentoring relationship. In those very rare occasions where I became aware of such intent in a mentee, I would make it very clear that I would not focus my time or energy on that outcome. While promotion might result from personal growth through mentoring, and while I would always be open to sharing my network with my mentees, my focus is always on holistic personal growth and development.

Finally, I would offer that mentoring is not the answer to a "challenging" boss. Each of us has probably had that experience at least once in our careers and we needed a shoulder to cry on or a sounding board to vent. While a mentor can provide invaluable support in terms of providing perspective, I have always found it best to turn the mentee toward resolution within his or her chain of command/formal organizational structure.

If you are a mentor and get caught up in one of these circumstances, I would recommend that you listen, allow the mentee to vent, then gently prod him or her to have a meaningful private conversation with the boss to work the issue. The leader is often the last to know there is a problem and the mentee is hesitant to bring it up. Point the mentee in the right direction – back to the boss where expectations can be exchanged candidly, and leveled, as they should be. Getting yourself in the middle of these situations will never lead to a good outcome; you may become so caught up in the drama that you become a problem to both the mentee and the boss.

### The Trap of the "Brilliant" Answer

Over the years, I have come to believe that Mentor Intelligence™ is not about the mentor providing any answers to the mentee. This may seem counterintuitive – isn't mentoring about the mentor providing guidance based on wisdom and years of experience? In my early years I probably thought that was true. Now after experiencing many more mentoring successes and failures, I don't think that any more.

Several years ago, I attended a Kellogg Innovation Network (KIN) meeting in Chicago.[1] During a lunch break, I had the privilege of sitting next to a wonderful leader named Betsy Holden. Betsy is the former Co-CEO of Kraft Foods. We talked about the challenge of changing cultures in large organizations. Betsy reflected on something that she learned as an elementary school teacher before she started working at Kraft. She said that we are so often driven to the brilliant answer that we do not take the time or energy to ask the right questions. As a compulsive problem solver, I was captivated by her words. Of course, she was right. Time after time I had seen this play out, most especially when the world was crashing around us and getting the right answer to the right question was so very critical and urgent.

Her insight was life changing. I reflected on her words, and adopted the concept in my mentoring practice. Rather than offering my mentees answers that I did not have to live with, I

---

[1] Kellogg Innovation Network (KIN) is a platform founded by Robert C. Wolcott and Mohan Sawhney for on-going collaboration between Kellogg faculty, corporate innovation leaders, non-profits and government...to promote innovation led growth. [Extract from *Kellogg.campusgroups.com/kin/about*]

began to focus on exploratory questions designed to surface options and alternatives for their consideration and decision. Taking my personal ego out of the equation and focusing solely on the mentee's situation put the mentee squarely in the driver's seat, with my role as a navigator to reflect choices and consequences.

This questions-based approach to mentoring has delivered solid results, and in the process, strengthened my skills as a mentor and as a leader. As I considered my own early experiences, I realized that the best mentoring I received throughout my career came from mentors who had deep skills at asking probing questions and identifying consequences rather than directing me to their personally preferred solutions.

## *A Blueprint for Exploring Possibilities*

(1) A baseline, working definition of Mentor Intelligence™ for conventional mentorship is a process with a deliberate focus on relationship and mutual sharing of knowledge, access and perspectives. Reverse mentorship is a powerful notion where any mentor who is open to learning from his or her mentee's experiences, perspectives or insights can find sustained personal growth.

(2) There is another, perhaps more powerful and applicable type of mentorship that is not about rank, senior-subordinate relationships, or power, but rather focused on equal mutually beneficial relationships. This type of mentorship is especially relevant for those in non-traditional organizations and emerging generations who do not live or work with the constraints of conventional hierarchical organizations.

(3) Regardless of type of mentorship, the tools, techniques and perspectives of Mentor Intelligence™ are valuable and applicable beyond conventional mentoring situations.

(4) Experiential lessons-learned, both personal and organizational, highlight approaches that can cause mentoring to be ineffective or fail completely:

- It is not about fixing someone or something.
- It is not about re-making a mentee into your image and likeness.
- It is not about creating pro-forma programs, quotas or elitist programs that only benefit a small group of exclusive leaders.
- It is not the answer to a promotion or a challenging boss.

(5) The most effective mentoring is not about providing answers, but rather, about offering focused, clarifying questions to develop options and to understand consequences. This is important because it allows the mentor to serve as a guide to alternatives and consequences, keeps the mentee in the driver's seat, and ensures that the mentor is providing life skills to the mentee rather than serving as a "problem solver."

*Chapter Two Practical Exercise*
*Questions For Personal Reflection and Growth*

1. Have you ever experienced an effective mentoring relationship either as a mentor or a mentee? What distinguished it from other relationships? Why did it work? Can you characterize success factors?

2. Have you ever had a bad experience either as a mentor or mentee? What happened? How did it affect your relationship with that person?

3. Have you ever had a mentor try to "fix" you or tell you what you should be or do in a particular situation? How did that make you feel? Did you tell your mentor? What was the result?

4. Does your current organization have a mentor program? In your opinion, how is it working? Who does it serve? How would you make it better?

## Chapter Three:  Mentoring for Life

### *The Waste of Good Intentions*

In my life I have been blessed with good mentorship and learned what separates good mentoring from bad mentoring. Every mentor has his or her own approach to being effective. Frankly, any process or technique that meets the needs of a mentee is good.  For those of you who are still trying to become better mentors, the following ideas might help.  Keep in mind that in the end, the only thing that really matters is what you do about mentorship, not what you say or think or hope for.  Organizational battlefields are strewn with the waste of good intentions.

Successful mentorship is the product of study, thought, practice and learning.  It is about action, not desire.  It is a discipline and as with any other discipline, it can become a way of being, a lifestyle that distinguishes the mentor.  As we used to say in the Army, soldiers may doubt what you say, but they will never doubt what you do.  There is no tool more powerful or effective in any leader's toolbox than personal example.

## *Investing for the Future*

For mentorship to be effectual, it has to be voluntary, both on the side of the mentor and mentee. If it is not voluntary on one or both sides, the relationship will likely begin with anger or resentment; hardly the way to grow close. I knew a senior leader who was directed to get an executive coach. He did so, and within a few months, he joked about how he chased his coach off (for the third time). In another instance, I was asked to pick up a particular mentee, and so I did. After a year of trying to make it work, I terminated the relationship when I found his efforts were geared more on attempts to use our relationship to work around his organizational leadership, instead of creating a positive mentoring relationship. While directed mentor situations are occasionally unavoidable, expectations for success should be held very low. That said, with focused effort using the tools and techniques in this book, I believe with the implementation of Mentor Intelligence™, it is possible to create win-win situations even in these circumstances

So let's consider the opposite situation, where an organization makes mentorship voluntary. In this case, a person seeks out a mentor and asks if they are able to make the time for them, no fault on both sides. It's easy to believe that such situations will typically have happy outcomes, but that is not always the case. Too often senior leaders either do not believe they have the time for meaningful mentoring, or they simply don't like to do it, so they put it at the bottom of the action pile.

Ironically, many of these executives rose through the ranks because someone mentored them. Now that they are in key positions and have the opportunity to pay their mentor debts back, they choose otherwise. Imagine what would happen if most of the senior leadership of an organization similarly opts out of mentoring? What would that mean to the organization?

What kind of culture results from that view of leadership? Is that the kind of organization that you want to work for or belong to? Probably not, if you have a choice!

The inescapable fact is that mentorship is a basic component of good leadership. I do not believe you can be a good leader if you are not a good mentor. Why? Because leaders, real leaders, don't just make things happen in a vacuum. They protect the organization's future by growing the next generation of leaders so the organization lives beyond their tenure. Successful organizational leaders operate in the present and in the future. They invest time, talent and energy in both dimensions so the organization can appreciate sustained growth over time. In so doing, they create a legacy of success that lives on in the lives of their mentees.

### *The Central Paradox*

If on one hand mentorship must be voluntary to be effective, and on the other it is a basic responsibility of every leader in every organization, how can these competing concepts be reconciled? There is a solution.

If every leader in an organization wants to mentor and does so without having to be told, the problem is solved. If a leader wants to mentor, no one has to tell them how important it is to the lifeblood of the organization or make them do it. If there are organizational leaders who do not want to mentor, they should be mentored themselves until they understand this as a basic leader responsibility. Fear of mentoring is often driven by lack of experience, lack of support, or lack of training. Given the right coaching and the right tools these reluctant mentors can be grown to their full potential as leaders and mentors. If they are given the opportunity to grow and still resist, they should be replaced. The only way to create a vibrant, effective culture of mentorship is to establish the expectation at the top and drive it through every layer of the organization.

An organization that excuses any person in a leadership position from growing the next generation of leaders mortgages its future. Companies are in business for profit and continuity – make money today and tomorrow. It's not enough to get half of that right. It makes absolutely no sense from a competitive advantage point of view, and it represents such a waste of human capital.

### *A Special Word For Technical and Functional Leaders*

In some organizations leaders may be selected based primarily on their technical or functional expertise, not on their leadership skills. The more senior of these leaders may have hundreds if not thousands of employees who depend on their leadership for development, guidance and mentorship. If these leaders do not step up to that challenge for whatever reason, their subordinates are left to fend for themselves. The leader may have underdeveloped mentorship skills or simply just not be comfortable relating to others. The reason really does not matter; no excuse is worth the cost to the organization. It is a basic leader responsibility to grow those critical skills and to devote the time and energy to mentoring their teams.

This situation is not just limited to technical fields. It impacts teams and employees in every type of business, academia and government. No organization is immune. Leaders who have undeveloped or underdeveloped mentoring skills can create deeply rooted self-sustaining mentor voids wherever they pass.

My encouragement is for senior leaders of every type of organization and every team to invest whatever resources it takes to create viable, sustained leader development programs to include mentorship training. The investment will pay dividends in terms of sustained performance, increased employee satisfaction, and improved quality of life for everyone on the team.

### *The Only Standard That Counts Is The One You Choose To Enforce*

So what is the answer to creating a sustained culture of mentorship in any organization or team? I think we make this too hard. It really is as simple as the key leaders declaring that mentorship is a basic expectation of every leader, no exceptions. If you don't know how to mentor or it makes you uncomfortable, keep reading - I can teach you! If you don't want to learn or you simply don't want to do it, don't expect to be compensated like the leaders who take this responsibility seriously and understand that it is the life-blood of our organization. The only standard that counts is the one you choose to enforce – the rest is just talk. If senior organizational leaders are tentative on mentorship, it will never rise to meet the need.

If every organization were to adopt a model of mentorship where it is a basic expectation at every level, I suspect their human capital would grow significantly creating a competitive advantage in the process. Why in the world would any key leader marginalize any resource that could make the difference between survival and failure, especially when it involves skills that can be taught and learned? If you want good mentorship, demand it at every level, expect it at every level, and reward it at every level. It is the ultimate win-win-win solution. The organization wins with increased competitive advantage, the employee wins with life-long life-giving relationships, and the mentors win with all the benefits that accrue from serving others and learning in the process.

## The Right "Soup"

Good mentorship programs, without exception, create, nurture and grow meaningful relationships. As with all relationships, this is about taking a chance on a person and committing your resources to help and support them. It is about investment of time, of energy, and yes, of resources, to help the mentee.

Talk to anyone who has ever had the privilege of having a real mentor and I bet they tell you that they are still in touch with that person. They likely became life friends long after they moved away from one another. You will hear stories still vivid today about how that mentor took them under their wing and took a chance on them when no one else would. You will hear stories about how the mentor created expanded growth opportunities, shared both experience and wisdom and helped the mentee through significant challenges and troubled times. You are very likely to hear the word "family" come up – the mentor is "like another member of the family."

Underpinning all of this, there will be reflections about how the mentor committed himself to the mentee and invested in the mentee's life. The words "trust," "mutual respect" and "support" come up because there are no better words to describe what happens in an effective mentor-mentee relationship. It really becomes clear as to why mentorship can be so effective at eliminating isolation. At its very core is the care and concern of one human being for another, free of judgment and free of expectation. This is the "right soup" for growth for a lifetime!

## Does Chemistry Matter?

Previously, I mentioned the word "chemistry" in the context of how a mentor might assess a mentee. I stated the danger if a mentor only selects mentees who fit the mentor's "mold" and the possible impact on diversity and inclusion. Here is the other side of the coin. I have entered hundreds of mentee relationships, and it is a fact that there is such a thing as "chemistry" and it plays a significant role in effective mentoring. Each of us is drawn to those who are most like us – it is not unnatural that we would each reach out to those who remind us of ourselves.

I have two cautions. The one already discussed is that if the mentor is too narrowly focused to the extent that only people like him/her are acceptable as mentees, diversity and inclusion both suffer. This really is a subtle form of discrimination as a mentor denies the benefits of mentorship to those who are "different." While no one can tell you whom you should mentor, just make sure you are keeping both your mind and your door open to the possibility. The second caution is certainly one we all know, but it bears repeating. First impressions can sometimes prove wrong, and if the mentor makes a snap decision about lack of chemistry and chooses to turn down a request, both mentor and mentee may lose out on what could be a profoundly rewarding experience. What may seem "real" at the first session may appear totally different after a little more investment in trust and relationship building.

My view is simply this – don't ever say no to a mentee request unless there is some ethical or moral issue surrounding your decision. If a mentee seeks you out, odds are they see something in you that can help them, and it's worth your time to explore the connection. Chemistry can be a late bloomer, and what a shame it would be to prematurely reject what could eventually be a life changing experience.

Far more important ingredients in the mix are candor, honesty and integrity. While chemistry has a lot to do with personality style and can unfold as the mentee and mentor both grow, candor, honesty and integrity are perceptible from the outset.

More importantly they are extremely hard to fake. A few direct questions from the mentor about why the mentee seeks this mentor relationship will provide the answer. I find it particularly effective to sit at 90 degrees to the mentee and look into their eyes when I ask the questions such as "Why did you seek me out," "What help are you seeking from me," and "How would you define success in our mentor relationship." These provide a reasonably good start. It only happens rarely to me, but on occasion, I will pick up something that causes me to question a mentee's motive. When I do, I find it best to lay my concerns on the table and talk them out frankly. That is far better than pretending that everything is fine, not asking the tough questions and leaving the session with doubt.

### *Developing Mentor Intelligence*™

Perhaps one of the most important experiential insights I have gained from my years of mentoring is the notion that there is such a thing as "Mentor Intelligence™." This is a similar notion to emotional intelligence[2] and it is a composite of inspiration, discernment, judgment, active listening, perception, empathy, and systems thinking (understanding the interconnectedness of most things in life). It is about making connections that the mentee is not able to make, and making the connections meaningful to the mentee.

There is a useful military counterpart. In Carl von Clausewitz's masterpiece *"On War,"* he discusses a powerful concept called Coup d'oeil in a chapter on military genius. Coup d'oeil is the commander's "inward eye" that allows "quick recognition of the truth that the mind would ordinarily miss or would perceive only after long study and reflection."[3]

---

[2] Goleman, D. (1988). Working With Emotional Intelligence. New York: Bantam Books

[3] Carl Von Clausewitz, On War, edited and translated by Michael Howard

39

This is the unique insight derived from intelligence, experience and ability to draw connections, the very same ingredients comprising Mentor Intelligence™. In mentoring, Mentor Intelligence™ allows the mentor to quickly gain a sense of the "terrain" impacting the mentee's situation, analyze it, and discern the truth within it. As with Coup d'oeil, Mentor Intelligence™ can be developed through experience and effort.

Mentorship that centers on focused, relevant questions from the mentor to the mentee, presented in a nonjudgmental, non-threatening way, is key to the magic of possibilities. It is not about the mentor giving the mentee answers, regardless of how tempting that might be. Recognize that the more significant your questions become, the more difficult they may be for the mentee to answer. Honor that by acknowledging it. It is not unusual for a mentee to feel lost and out of control as they struggle to understand their life circumstances. If this happens remind the mentee that they really are in control of the process, that there are always multiple outcomes to any situation, and that you are present to listen, reflect, and help sort through the choices and consequences. In subsequent chapters, I will show you how to do this in a non-judging but guiding way that creates deep trust and confidence.

It is really important as a mentor that you don't appear to "have all the answers," because you don't and because you don't have to live with any that you offer. Support, guide, probe, and explore – these are the tenets of good mentorship, and I believe are the qualities you would all hope to have in a mentor were you in the mentee's shoes. In this way, mentoring is both an art and a science. It is shaped by personal experiences, by successes, by failures, and above all, by adopting a larger systems view about actions and consequences.

---

and Peter Paret, Princeton University Press, 1976, p. 102

In time, mentors who adopt mentorship as a way of life will increase their Mentor Intelligence™ and develop the ability to form and apply the right kind of probing questions at the right time and to the right effect.  As with any discipline, the more you practice the more expertise you will gain, the more Mentor Intelligence™ you will build, and the more comfortable you will become with the art and science of mentorship.

### *What Does Right Look Like?*

When I was a young Captain in the Army I was privileged to command my first unit, an organization with approximately 120 soldiers. We had been a peacetime Army for the last several years.  During a training exercise my new commander paid us a visit.  He asked me several critical questions about why my unit and I were doing certain things a certain way, and I offered him the stock answer that we were following the higher unit's standard operating procedures.  He asked me a single question that shaped my command philosophy and my Army life – "Would you do it this way in combat operations?"

He was a combat veteran and from his war experiences understood the difference between form and substance.  Even though I had not served in combat at that time, I immediately knew the answer – "No Sir, I would not!"  His response was simple – "Then don't do it in peacetime operations."  He did not qualify the answer, nor did he appear concerned that his advice was counter to our higher brigade level unit's guidance. I got a real lesson in courage that day.  He told me that anyone could take soldiers into combat, but that it took real leaders to bring them home alive.

I carried that message with me in my leadership philosophy from that day forward, to include a battalion command of over 700 soldiers, two deployments to the Middle East, and one to Kosovo.  Of course, he was right. For the first time in my military life, I really knew what right looked like, and I began to understand that my responsibility as a mentor was to make that message part of every one of my soldier's lives.

This was not about pleasing higher headquarters. It was about doing the right thing for the right reasons each time and every time. That was what right looked like, and it shaped my mentoring in the military for the next few thousand soldiers. Note that he did not tell me what to do; he simply asked me a discerning question and let *me* decide what to do. That is what good mentorship looks like, and it is a fine example of good Mentor Intelligence™ in action.

### *A Life Gift That Keeps Giving*

More recently, one of my mentees called me very upset about a challenge she was having with her work team. I cleared my calendar to meet with her, listened to her concerns, and rather than focus on the specifics of that situation, I reframed the conversation to create a broader context. I talked about a document I had written years before called "My Letter To Me." My inspiration was a song by country artist Brad Paisley called "Letter To Me," a reflection on all the life lessons he would tell himself as a teenager if he could go back in time.[4] I had been asked by an early career group to give them a presentation on the lessons I had learned over my work life. This single chart (Appendix A) was the result.

By sharing this with my mentee, I diverted her focus from the temporary work challenges and frustrations to the larger questions of life. She was so moved by the work that when we met the next time to review the situation, she opened her book and presented me with her very own version of "My Letter to

---

[4] Brad Paisley, "Letter to Me," *5th Gear*, (Nashville: Arista Nashville, 2007).

Me," a beautiful reflection on all the goodness in her life and on the things that are most important to her. If the story stopped there it would be powerful enough for inclusion in this section, but it has taken on even deeper relevance in her life and in the lives of others around her.

Almost a year later my mentee was asked to share some personal insight with her colleagues at an internal team meeting. After much soul searching and internal debate about what to share, she found the courage to present her deeply moving and personal letter to every member of her team. Her candor, openness, and courageous sharing touched many of the members of her team including her team leaders. By becoming vulnerable to them and sharing something so personal, she created new possibilities for deeper, more meaningful relationships across the team. This is a powerful example of how good mentorship can create life-giving opportunities that ripple far beyond the life of the mentor and the mentee. It is a beautiful, elegant way to change the world one life at a time.

## *A Blueprint for Exploring Possibilities*

(1) Good mentoring must begin willingly on the part of both mentor and mentee.
(2) Mentoring is a basic component of good leadership. It should be a basic expectation of every organizational leader. Every leader should want to mentor and should do so because it is the right thing to do. If they do not know how they should be held accountable for learning. No leader should ever be excused from this responsibility.
(3) Mentorship at its most basic level is about relationship founded on trust and understanding based on candor, honesty and integrity. It takes time and investment. It also takes courage on part of both mentor and mentee.
(4) Effective mentoring hinges on the mentor's ability to ask non-judging, clarifying questions that present possibilities

and frame consequences, rather than on providing answers that the mentor does not have to live with. It is about reinforcing the fact that the mentee is truly in the driver's seat to decide life's most pressing questions and own the resulting decisions.

(5) Mentor Intelligence™ is a basic component of effective leadership involving experiential insight, active listening skills, active mutual support, and productive empathy. It is also about seeing and understanding the "inter-connectedness" of everything – a systems view of life – and sharing that view with others. As with any skill set, the more you practice mentor skills, the better you will become at mentoring and the more you will grow your Mentor Intelligence™.

(6) If nurtured and sustained, mentor relationships can transcend time and distance. They can last a lifetime, enriching not only the lives of both mentee and mentor, but changing the world in the process as the gift is shared, paid forward, and paid back.

*Chapter Three Practical Exercise*
*Questions For Personal Reflection and Growth*

1. Have you ever had a negative mentoring experience, either as a mentee or mentor? How did you turn that situation into something positive? Did it encourage you or discourage you from mentoring someone yourself?

2. Have you ever been asked by someone to serve as a mentor and turned them down because you were too busy? Did you offer any other alternative to help that person?

3. How are you helping your work organization mentor early career employees? Is this something you expect of yourself as a leader? If your organization has a formal mentor program, what are you doing to support it?

4. When you think about the most effective leaders you have observed, how did they set a positive example of mentorship? What did they do that set them apart? How can you make that a part of your personal leadership?

5. Have you ever rejected a person or distanced yourself from that person because they were "different"? What were you afraid of? How can you grow as a leader and a mentor by running toward the differences rather than running away from them?

6. Have you ever experienced a mentor who demonstrated "coup d'oeil" or significant levels of Mentor Intelligence™? What were the skills that the mentor demonstrated? How can you incorporate them into your own personal mentorship style?

# Chapter Four: Putting Mentorship Into Practice

Productive mentoring depends on effective and receptive mentors and mentees. The premise of this book is that mentorship involves skills on both sides, skills that can be learned and can be taught. It is also a discipline that, when practiced, can increase anyone's Mentor Intelligence™ and effectiveness as both a mentor and a mentee. There is an old saying that you cannot know how to be a good leader until you have learned how to be a good follower. I believe the same applies to mentorship. It is not possible to be a good mentor until you have become a good mentee.

For those non-traditional mentor relationships where there is not a senior-subordinate relationship, I encourage both parties to follow the guidelines for <u>both</u> mentees and mentors presented below. More than anything else, this chapter is just about creating and adopting behaviors that create mutual respect and support. So let's get started on our journey!

### *First Steps...Preparation, Preparation, Preparation!*

Before asking someone to serve as a mentor for you, take the time to frame your thoughts and know what outcome you want from the relationship. Be deliberate and purposeful. Write your thoughts down – this will become the basic tool to frame and cross-level expectations once you decide whom you want to ask to become your mentor. Be honest with yourself. If you enter the relationship intentionally mindful of what you are asking of a mentor, you will have no difficulty explaining that in an authentic and personal way.

Every mentee has different needs and different reasons for seeking a mentor. For some, there is an urgent decision that the mentee needs immediate help with. For others, the need may be broader or more elusive. Whatever your reasons, take the time to document the top three outcomes you seek before you meet with your mentor. Doing the work upfront is not only an investment that will pay dividends as the relationship develops, but it also shows the mentor that you are sincere about wanting help and that you are willing to work for it.

What do you do if you are not sure about the specific outcomes you are seeking? Just think about the challenges you are currently facing and start with that list. For most of us, defining challenges is not hard to do and at the very least will give the mentor something to work with.

### *Picking A Mentor*

How do you pick a mentor? Choose carefully – do some research. As with any important life decision, taking the time to research the possibilities is certain to lead to a better outcome. I suggest augmenting whatever mentorship you are getting within your current leadership chain with a mentor outside that chain. This allows you to get different perspectives as well as connecting you to a different network. Even in the most mentor-barren organizations, pockets of excellence will exist for the determined mentee to find. Leverage your social and professional networks. They are the most powerful and effective tools to guide the search. Ask your friends and colleagues if they know any good mentors. Discuss it with your organizational leaders. Let them all know that you are seeking a mentor and explain the kind of person you are looking for. The more precisely you are able to define what you are looking for, the easier it is for others to help you. I recommend multiple mentors because different types of experience and expertise are needed. Good mentors work hard to be visible, especially in organizations where the need is greatest.

Once you decide whom to ask, be deliberate about how you ask. I have been approached over almost every media possible – emails, phone calls, drive-by office meetings, after presentations, hand-offs from other leaders, hand-offs from other mentees, the possibilities are endless. It really does not matter so long as the request is intentional and respectful. From my perspective, face-to-face is best, but that is not always possible. When you do ask, treat the mentor with the same courtesy that you would hope to be extended to you when you are asked to be a mentor. Don't apologize for asking, and don't fail to ask because you think the mentor is too busy. Good mentors treat mentoring as a primary leader responsibility, not an additional duty, and they will find a way to fit anyone in who is willing to work for the support.

### *Four Critical Behaviors for Mentees*

So now you have a new mentor! Congratulations! Where do you go from here? Here is a basic checklist of personal rules I would recommend that you follow as a considerate mentee:

**1. Be respectful of the mentor's time**. There is hardly anything more insulting to a mentor who has made the time for a meeting only to have the mentee pull out his cell phone and take a call. It is just not acceptable for either party, and the wise mentor would immediately cancel a session so the mentee can take the more important phone call.

Good mentors typically have many competing demands on their time. While mentoring is not a burden, it can get out of control if some basic protocols are not followed. I made my sessions self-regulating by allowing the mentee to drive the frequency with a very simple technique. If a mentee needed an appointment they would schedule it. If it was on my calendar, I did it. If it was not on my calendar, I would still try to meet with the mentee if there was some pressing need. That said, office drive-bys could be very disrupting so I suggest this approach be avoided if possible. By asking the mentee to be responsible for scheduling sessions, I was always able to accommodate anyone who wanted me to mentor them. It was a simple process and worked for everyone concerned.

**2. Do the work, follow the process, and be prepared.** Mentor sessions are not freewheeling conversations. Those are a waste of everyone's time. As a mentor, I respected the mentee's time as much as I expected the mentee to respect my time, and that required preparation on both sides. I have a process that involves homework (this will be discussed completely in the next chapter). Between sessions, I expect my mentees to do the assigned work so that we can have focused conversations that take advantage of the time available. The more prepared my mentees are, the better support I can provide them. By following a disciplined, structured process that I would explain in our very first face-to-face session, we both knew where we were headed at any given time, how we were going to get to the next steps, and what the expectations were at every session. A little structure can be a powerful enabler for both the mentee and the mentor so long as it does not become the end in and of itself. If something comes up that requires us to divert a session or two for a separate

49

conversation, we simply take that path and get back on track as soon as possible.

**3. Be present – dig deep, be candid, be authentic, make yourself vulnerable, and allow yourself to be uncomfortable**. Good mentorship depends fundamentally on identifying and framing opportunities that fit your needs as a mentee. The more open you are to feedback, to growth and to considering new possibilities, the more effective the mentoring will be. Bring your whole self into the dialogue. Be transparent, be honest, and challenge yourself. Know that the greatest personal growth is likely found in those spaces where you are most uncomfortable or challenged. The deeper you dig, the more exposed you will become, and that is why trust is such a fundamental characteristic of good mentorship. As with most meaningful things in life, the more you put into the relationship, the more you will get out of it. If you keep things superficial with your mentor, don't expect anything more than superficial results!

**4. Give it back!** Be grateful for your mentor and show your appreciation by learning how to become a mentor yourself. There is no greater reward to any mentor than having a mentee become a mentor to others in need.

### *Ten Critical Practices For <u>Mentors</u>*

Now we will turn the discussion to some thoughts on being a good mentor. Here is a summation of the ten best practices that I have found most useful and effective:

**1. Be gracious if asked** to be a mentor. It is a special honor and should be treated as such rather than as a burden.

**2. Set up an exploratory face-to-face meeting** with the mentee. Don't wait to do this – if you do, you may forget or your mentee may believe you really do not want to be a mentor. That is not a good way to begin a relationship. The first session should be a "no-fault" session with either side able to opt out if things do not work out. I previously discussed the issue with chemistry. Here I would simply say if it does not feel right, it probably isn't right. Be careful, however, to avoid making a rash decision. Here is where Mentor Intelligence™ can play a major role. Many of my initial sessions over the past several years were a little rough. That is to be expected, relationships take time and energy. If you stick to it, you may find your initial impressions are wrong. If things don't sort out by the end of the second session, it's probably time to tell the mentee that you think he or she should seek another mentor, then help them make that connection.

**3.   Treat the scheduled mentor time as a core leader responsibility**, not something you do when you have the time. I know of a few mentors whose administrative assistants would cancel mentee sessions month after month, often, I suspect, without the mentor's knowledge.   In one case a mentee got bumped six months in a row without a single meeting after the leader agreed to the mentor relationship. Cancelled sessions are unavoidable from time to time, but when they become the norm, it speaks volumes to a mentee about your real priorities. Leader actions will always speak louder than words.   Your personal example is the best way you can establish your credentials as a mentor. If mentorship is important to you, tell your staff.   The best way to avoid this type of problem is simply to track and manage mentor commitments yourself on a personal calendar rather than delegating it.   It really is that important.

**4.   Be respectful and be present.** There is nothing more disrespectful to a mentee than accepting a meeting then constantly looking at your watch or cell phone, or worse yet, working on your computer. Be respectful and be present –

make the time count. Demand the same from your mentees. One practical suggestion is simply to turn off all phones at the beginning of the session and take the temptation away.

**5. Meet anywhere but in your office**. This behavior is for traditional mentor-mentee situations. Mentorship is about relationship, not about position or power. Your office is a symbol of your authority regardless of your leadership style. Find another place where you can meet on level ground. If that is not possible, at least move away from behind your desk. Stories are legend of very senior leaders who are so insecure meeting with subordinates that they will not move from their positional power behind their desk. The message that sends – "I am in charge, you are not" - is just not appropriate for mentoring.

**6. Resist the temptation to provide answers.** This critical thread has been woven throughout this book because it is so important and so difficult. This is especially true when a distraught mentee is asking you for your advice. No matter how strongly you may feel about the options, you will not have to live with the consequences if the mentee follows your advice. Develop the situation through non-judgmental, clarifying questions that center around the mentee's needs and circumstances, not yours. Use the questions to surface possibilities they might not have thought of on their own. Brainstorm alternatives and use your Mentor Intelligence™ to probe, guide and suggest. Offer your mentee the wisdom of your experience, and even your lessons learned, but let them come up with the answers that will work best for them. By allowing the mentee to "own it" all, you set the stage for growth and learning. There is no better place to learn than in the driver's seat, and if you take that role you will deny your mentee the experience and both lose in the process.

**7. Challenge your mentee to dig deep and become uncomfortable**. In the previous section we discussed how important it is for the mentee to be vulnerable to you and to trust that growth will result. As a mentor, you need to be aware of the impact of your questions and challenges on the mentee. Many times, facing into our deepest insecurities is the quickest path to finding new opportunities. With sensitive, gentle guidance you can make those possibilities real. It is normal during these sessions for the mentee to become emotional. The worst thing you can do as a mentor is to overreact or show discomfort when that happens. Challenge, guide and probe, but above all, support your mentee with empathy and constructive compassion. It is even more powerful when you as a mentor allow yourself to be vulnerable to your mentee. Share your failures and disappointments candidly and openly. As you do, your mentees will follow suit.

**8. Tell your stories.** While it is not helpful for you to tell the mentee what to do, it is extremely valuable for you to share your life experiences and lessons. Take risk, share both good and bad, names omitted of course! By being vulnerable and exposing your own life challenges, you encourage the mentees to do the same and they will respond in kind. The trust that is the underpinning of all good relationships must be a two-way street. Use your life experiences to illuminate *choices and consequences*, explore them fully in the context of the mentee's current situation and focus on exploring all the possibilities. In doing so, you will broaden the mentee's perceptions about how much control he or she has over any situation.

**9. Be open to learning from your mentees and tell them so.** The process of reverse mentoring is an extremely powerful concept. Mentors who presume to have all the experience, knowledge and wisdom shut themselves off to the enrichment that comes from listening to, and learning from the experience, knowledge and wisdom of their mentees. This is especially true where different generations come together and perspectives on any single topic can be so diverse. If you allow yourself to learn, rest assured the mentee will be more than willing to accept the offer. Some of the most significant lessons and insights in my life have come from reverse mentoring.

**10. Be an advocate.** Share the unique resources that you have due to your organizational position and life experiences (your access, network, contacts, credibility, organizational knowledge, lessons learned, etc.). The beauty of real mentor-mentee relationships lies in the mentor's sharing those resources to benefit the mentee's life. Your mentees sought you out because they believed that you had something of significance to offer them. Making these gifts available to them can change their lives forever, and give your life significance in the process. This is truly noble giving – the more you give, the more you will get in return.

## *A Blueprint for Exploring Possibilities*

(1) Effective mentorship requires productive and receptive mentors and mentees. There are skills that can be mastered for both. These guidelines apply as much to non-traditional mentor relationships as they do to traditional mentor relationships.
(2) Chose your mentor or mentor-partner wisely; research your options, expand your network and grow! Choose from outside your current direct organizational leadership, if possible.
(3) Learning how to be a good mentee involves a number of behaviors to include being respectful of the mentor's time, being prepared by doing the work ahead of time, being present and vulnerable during the sessions, and being open to new perspectives and opportunities. It also means

paying it back by learning how to mentor others in return for the gift you have been privileged to receive.

(4) Learning how to be a good mentor means first learning how to be a good mentee. For reference, I've provided ten critical mentor behaviors that will maximize your Mentor Intelligence™. They can be learned by anyone willing to invest the time and energy to become better at the art and science of mentorship.

*Chapter Four Practical Exercise*
*Questions For Personal Reflection and Growth*

1. If you have a mentor how did you decide on whom to ask? How did you prepare for the first session? How did it go?

2. What did you learn as a mentee? Was the relationship based on questions or answers? What expectations did you have and how were they met?

3. Have you ever served as a mentor? How did you feel when you were asked? How did you approach the challenge? What mistakes did you make and what did you learn from the experience?

4. When you reviewed the ten practices for being an effective mentor, what did you think about them? Do you believe that these ten behaviors capture what it takes to be a good mentor? Have you tried others that you would add to the list?

5. Have you ever had a mentor serve as an advocate for you? What did they do? What did it do for you? What did you learn?

# Chapter Five: The ALtuitive Method - A Five-Step Framework for Creating Life Strategies

### *Tying The Pieces Together*

Mentorship is a very personal journey. We each bring our unique skills and experiences to the table. Over the last few years of my mentorship practice, I began to believe that there was a deeper possibility to the discipline. By integrating strategic planning processes into mentoring, we could take mentoring to a higher level, empowering mentor relationships, creating life strategies, and increasing Mentor Intelligence™ in the process for both the mentor and the mentored. The benefits of this strategic approach have universal application. Whether you are an individual seeking greater control over your life, or part of a traditional or progressive mentor relationship, you can learn these techniques to create personal life strategies and grow as individuals and leaders. My approach is rooted in three special concepts that have provided the most significant insights in my own life.

## The Whole Person Foundation

In the first chapter I introduced the whole person concept, the notion that each of us is a composite of mind, body and spirit. I have had the opportunity to experience, and appreciate, the power of this fundamental concept in both my personal and professional life. Embracing it gives each of us the opportunity to experience integrity (wholeness) in a more complete, holistic and practical way.

It has special significance in creating personal life strategies because it provides the critical foundation on which everything else depends. To be a complete person, we have to be whole in each - mind, body and spirit. The three parts are interlinked. What happens in one part of a person's life affects the whole person. Sometimes, just giving voice to a mentee's whole person can be liberating, providing rich insight and context into the things that are going on in that person's life.

## Understanding Life's Larger Questions

The second insight is related, and also has important application beyond its initial purpose to the practice of mentoring. In 2000, I was deployed to Kosovo as part of a NATO Peace Keeping force. It was during this deployment that I came face to face with the horrific human toll of ethnic genocide. The atrocities committed by both sides in the conflict were mind, and spirit, numbing. In anger, sadness and frustration, I sought solace by seeking counsel from in a very special Army chaplain named Tim Bedsole. To this day, I carry a 3x5 card with special quotes from special people who have touched my life. Tim is one of those people. In one of our many intentional conversations about life, Tim told me that until a person answers the "big" questions in life, the "little" questions are just not going to make any sense.

What a simple, but elegant insight! Through deep personal experience I have found that it applies to almost any aspect of a person's life. When connected to the whole person concept, it becomes a powerful guiding concept for any mentor. On many occasions a mentee would ask me to help them, yet the issue they were trying to work through involved one or more of the "little" questions. By focusing the mentee on the "bigger" life questions, we were able to create a more meaningful framework for sorting through the various options and opportunities. It made our conversations easier, richer and more productive. Helping a mentee understand the bigger life questions underlying each issue creates context for building effective life strategies.

### The Answers Embedded In Life Questions

In chapter two I introduced Betsy Holden's concept of focusing on the right questions rather than providing "brilliant" answers. Spending the time and energy to explore any situation through focused, non-judging, clarifying questions is a sound investment in any relationship, mentor or otherwise. The seemingly brilliant answer to the wrong question represents a waste of precious resources both for the mentor and the mentee. Getting the mentee to the right question where even a partially right answer can be found moves the mentee in the right direction and opens the door to meaningful solutions. This concept is ideally suited for life strategy mentoring where there is never a single possible answer. Probing for the right questions can help the mentee understand all the viable alternatives as well as the consequences of each, leading to a better outcome.

### The Sum Is Greater Than The Parts

By applying these concepts to a unique personal strategic planning methodology, I have been able to help my mentees create meaningful life strategies. There are five sequential steps in this process as shown in Figure 5.1 on the next page. The rest of this chapter will guide you through each of them. While they are not difficult, reviewing this section several times will yield big dividends as you learn how the pieces complement each another and form a complete package. Mastering this process can increase your Mentor Intelligence™ while giving you a practical way to help your mentees find the future they deserve. As an added benefit, learning these steps as a mentor allows you to apply them to your life as well. It is very powerful for the mentee to see that you are willing to do this work for yourself as well. For those who are engaged in non-traditional mentor relationships, the terms "mentee" and "mentor" are interchangeable with "mentor partner."

---

ALtuitive Holdings, LLC

## Building Life Strategies Through Mentoring

- Step 1: Creating relationship and defining expectations
- Step 2: Self Awareness - creating the context for life strategies through a Personal Asset Inventory (PAI)
- Step 3: Building a Personal Development Timeline – looking forward and backward in time to frame opportunity space and to imagine desired future state(s)
- Step 4: Developing Personal Life Strategies – using a disciplined incremental approach to creating opportunity space and to achieving life goals
- Step 5: Executing the Discipline – taking deliberate actions to create accountability and move ahead one step at a time

---

Figure 5.1 Building Life Strategies Through Mentoring

## *Step One: Creating Relationship and Defining Expectations*

As quickly as possible after someone asks you to be a mentor set up this first critical exploratory session. The longer you wait to set this meeting, the more doubt you sow about your willingness to take on the challenge. I suggest scheduling the meeting the same day that you are asked and holding the meeting within the following two weeks as a good rule of thumb. If that is not possible, contact the person who made the request and explain your timeline to remove any doubt or concern they may have.

Before the first meeting ask the mentee to provide you with the top three things he or she wants you to work with them over the next several months. That allows both of you to think about the relationship and define expectations. To conduct the meeting, find a comfortable private place (use common sense) outside of your office if possible, and be sensitive to the mentee's concerns (if any) about being seen as a mentee. In some circles, a person's desire to be mentored might be seen as a sign of weakness. It's usually best to ask about such sensitivities before picking a location.

Schedule the first meeting for no more than one hour. At that meeting, you should review whatever ground rules you may want to follow. Ask for the mentee's commitment in addition to giving the mentee yours. This first exploratory session seeks joint commitment for the journey by openly sharing mutual expectations and understanding motivations on both sides.

If you choose to use a process such as this one, take the time to carefully review it with the mentee. If the mentee wants to start working issues or concerns, I would caution them that you offer **relationship mentoring** rather than solutions. It is far more important to develop a relationship from which problems can be worked rather than diving in without doing the pre-work.

Occasionally someone would approach me to help them work through an issue with less than a week before they had to make a major decision. Things do happen and the mentee may have no control over the situation. In such cases I did my best to give them the initial help they were looking for while stressing the need for the longer-term relationship-based process. Good mentoring takes time and investment like most good things in life.

At the end of the first session, the mentor and mentee should jointly arrive at a basic frequency for follow-on sessions. The mentee should take responsibility for scheduling the second and all follow-on sessions. I have also found it very effective to assign "homework" for the mentee to accomplish before the next session, normally related to the next step in the process. This not only keeps us focused and on track, but also sets the expectation that mentoring with me is about work, not just talk.

## Step Two: Self-Awareness

Each of us has a "brand." In truth, we all have more than one and some have several of them! A personal brand is simply how others perceive you. I have often found that how a person wants to be perceived, and frankly how they perceive themselves, are at odds with what others think about them. Step two is about helping the mentee close that gap.

Gaining authentic self-awareness is a lifetime task. How each of us perceives our personality, the impact we have on others, and how our actions reflect our desired self-image or contrast with it, are all food for thought and reflection. The answers to these questions also help establish the critical context within which the "larger" questions make the most sense. The good news is that there is a lot of help available to anyone who wants to take the first step!

### *Leading The Person That You Are*

There are many different instruments available to aid both mentor's and mentee's journey toward self-discovery. If you have not done so, consider taking the Myers-Briggs Type Indicator® (MBTI®) instrument.[5] One of the most eye-opening initial self-awareness insights is just knowing that there are 16 basic personality profiles and that your own profile is not better or worse than any of the other 15 profiles. It is about differences, not values. Understanding how powerful our personality preferences are in creating personal brand image can be a huge step forward in self-awareness and an incredible leadership tool for teams and individuals. Books such as *Type Talk At Work* by Otto Kroeger, Janet Thuesen and Hile Rutledge, and *Please Understand Me* by David Keirsey and Marilyn Bates are wonderful introductions to the topic. The insights they provide are as valuable on the home front as they are at work.

There are many other useful instruments to include the Kirton Adaption-Innovation (KAI) Inventory[6] and literally dozens of leader style inventories available on the web. After years of working on teams and with highly educated adults, it still surprises me that so many have never even heard of any of these basic personality tools much less used one. You cannot begin to effectively lead or mentor others until you have learned how to lead the person that you are.

---

[5] See The Myers & Briggs Foundation web site:
http://www.myersbriggs.org/my-®®®-personality-type/mbti-basics/.
[6] See Kirton Adaption-Innovation Inventory web site: www.kaicentre.com.

## *A Strategist's Basic Tool*

After taking the first steps toward self-awareness, it's time to move on to the next tool. One of the most profound life-lessons that I have learned is the importance of Strengths, Weaknesses, Opportunities, and Threats (SWOT) analysis as the critical foundation of any strategy work, personal or otherwise. Without it, you are likely to build a strategy on a bed of sand. Since the work we are about is building life strategies, I created an instrument to develop a "living" personal SWOT - a snapshot in time that can be refined as life circumstances change and as your mentee grows. I call this tool a Personal Asset Inventory (PAI), which is a modification of the simple strengths/weaknesses analysis. While my experience has been that few of my mentees have completed an MBTI® or KAI, most people have been exposed to a simple strengths/weaknesses analysis at some point in their career.

My wife's father first exposed me to the basic idea early in my career. I was struggling with a job decision so I asked for his help. He had me take a sheet of paper, draw a horizontal line about an inch from the top, then draw a vertical line down the middle of the paper. On the left side he asked me to describe my strengths, on the right, my weaknesses. As simple as the tool was, it was still a valuable way for me to visualize my thoughts. I adopted the tool and adapted it to add some critical things missing from the basic design.

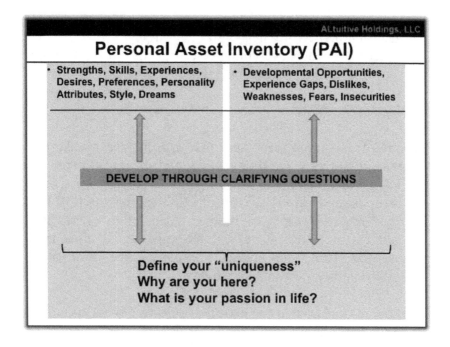

Figure 5.2 Personal Asset Inventory (PAI)

As Figure 5.2 illustrates, I expanded the categories to include skills, experiences, desires, preferences, styles, likes and dreams on the left (strengths) side, and developmental opportunities, experience gaps, dislikes, fears and insecurities to the right (weaknesses) side. The mentee builds this chart as homework and then I use it as a guide to explore answers to the three questions at the bottom of the chart. By augmenting the knowledge gained from this tool with other instruments and properly focused questions, I have been able to help my mentees define their uniqueness and better understand their personal passions in life and the values that underline them.

I believe that people are happiest when they are able to align their work life with their personal life. The process of revealing each mentee's specialness in these broader categories builds a solid foundation from which to evaluate any critical life decision and create meaningful life strategies. This is the base piece on which everything else depends, so we take the time to work it carefully and intentionally.

### Filling In The Gaps

At one of our initial meetings I ask each mentee to take this template and give it the time, energy and thought it deserves. By asking each mentee to document these areas, I am able to get them engaged in the fine art of self-awareness, a skill that will pay huge dividends over time. At a follow-on session, when the mentee presents me with the work, we devote at least one session, sometimes more, to exploring the information embedded in their personal answers.

Because I know that a person's self-awareness is often different than their desired brand, I also ask each mentee to give a 3x5" card to at least ten different people they know – friends, acquaintances, co-workers, family, even people the mentee believes dislikes them – and ask each person to provide three bullets (one phrase descriptors) that best define the mentee. By combining both the mentee's personal view of themselves with the view of ten or more external connections, I am able to get a much clearer picture of who this mentee really is, who they want to be, and what their "real" brand is.

Real self-awareness relies on both self-perception and on feedback from others. Both deserve consideration and both deserve a voice. By applying this technique for a number of years, I can state that each of my mentees has had at least one "aha!" moment from this process, learning something about themselves that they did not know before. Taking the time to work hard at self-discovery pays huge dividends in building relationship, creating the right environment for growth, and helping the mentee understand that mentorship involves work and growth, even when it is painful.

At the end of these initial sessions, the mentee will always have a more informed understanding of who they are, how others perceive them, and what their unique life gifts are. This all hinges on the mentor guiding the mentee through the process, the mentee doing the work, and both digging deep to discover why the mentee is here on this earth. If you serve as a mentor to another person and align their life decisions with their passion, their skills and attributes, their personal goals and aspirations, and their unique gifts, then you will have succeeded as a mentor.

As one of my first grade teachers explained to me, the greatest sin is not giving your special gifts the light of day. I thought that was one of the most profound life lessons I had ever heard, so I have used this as the end state of this phase of mentoring and found it to be life giving. Why am I here? Why am I unique? What is my unique value? What am I supposed to do with my life? As I reflect on my life learnings from Chaplain Tim Bedsole, these are indeed the larger questions of life, and they deserve our time, attention and focus.

## *Step 3: Building A Personal Development Timeline*

### *The 6" Putt!*

In the previous step I discussed self-awareness as the underpinning of all critical life decisions. In this section we will explore time using the game of golf to set the stage. I am a horrible golfer - I have a long list of helpful friends and colleagues who will be happy to verify that. I love the game. It just does not love me! What I did learn from playing golf is that it is a game of opposites and a game of psychology; that 6" putt counts as much as that "manly" 270 yard drive. If you cannot visualize the shot in your head, the chances of making it are next to nothing. Even as a beginner, if you can't shape the shot in your head it will not happen in your hands. The same holds true for almost any sport.

This next insight is so very important. If it's true in sports, what makes any of us think it is different in life? Any short or long-term future that you cannot visualize in your life will not happen, and left to its own devices, the decisions you make tomorrow will very closely parallel the ones you have made in you own life over the past several years. It's very easy to miss life's 6" putts over and over, just as it is to miss the long shots.

### *Einstein's Definition of Insanity*

So I designed a tool to capture both ends and the middle. It will help you to "shape your shot" to a desired future. Be honest with yourself, look backward at your life decisions and own them all, good and bad. If you want your future to look different than your past, something has to change. In a quote widely attributed to Albert Einstein, the definition of insanity is doing the same thing over and over again and expecting a different result.[7] By walking through the decisions you have made in the past and understanding why you made them, you can create a candid, authentic context to understand current and future decisions. "Those who cannot remember the past are condemned to repeat it"[8] and that applies as much to individuals as it does to nations!

---

[7] Albert Einstein, *(attributed)*, US (German-born) physicist (1879-1955)
[8] George Santayana, *Reason in Common Sense*, volume 1 of *The Life of Reason* (1905) Prometheus Books

## By The Numbers

Leveraging the hard work from the self-discovery sessions, I work with my mentees to create a Personal Development Timeline (Figure 5.3).

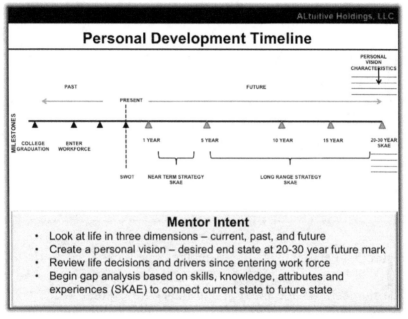

Figure 5.3 Personal Development Timeline

Most do this exercise on a single horizontal sheet of paper; however, one of my mentees put her timeline on a 10' roll so she could really explore and visualize the possibilities!

Let's walk through the process. If you are currently a mentor, I strongly encourage you to do one of these for your own life before using the tool with a mentee. You might be surprised at what you discover. If you do not have a mentor, don't wait for one. Take control of your life, grow your own Mentor Intelligence™, and then give others the gift of your learning.

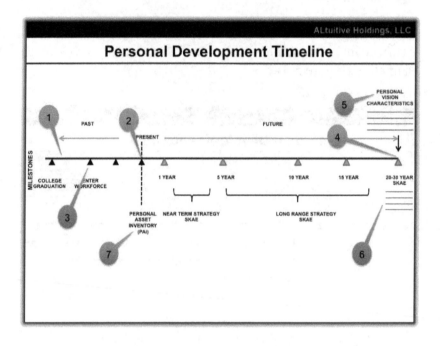

Figure 5.4 Personal Development Timeline Steps

The numbers on the chart (Figure 5.4) correspond to the text below:

1. Draw a simple horizontal line on a piece of paper.
2. On that line, add a point to represent the present. Make sure it is far enough to the right to allow listing the years and key life decisions that have taken place since entering the work force.
3. Add triangles to represent your key life decisions. During the timeline discussions, **we will work together to understand why you chose a certain direction or response.**
4. Visualize and characterize a successful life 25-30 years in the future. This is really where the fun begins! While

some mentees have a general idea about what direction they want to take their life, very few have ever taken the time to document it, much less, to build life strategic plans to achieve their goals.

5.  Describe your personal vision with concrete phrases such as, "independently wealthy," "married with children and grandchildren," "homeowner," "world traveller," "own my own business," "serving on a board of directors for a non-profit," "healthy," "spiritually fulfilled," "VP of a large company," whatever your dreams are made of. By giving the vision a voice we can start the process of building paths that will take them there. As life circumstances change, we revise the timeline.

6.  Define to the best of your ability the four categories – Skills, Knowledge, Attributes, and Experiences (SKAE)[9] – that would be required to live the life you want to live 25-30 years out. For example, if you want to be a small business owner, you need to have the basic business skills, knowledge of what it takes to own a business, the kind of personal attributes that are required to successfully start up and run a business, and some experiences that prepare you for the challenges you are likely to face. There is a smart power behind using the SKAE framework because it is a simple, useful tool to perform a career gap analysis.

7.  After following the previous six steps, take the time to review your current Personal Asset Inventory (PAI) developed in the previous phase. Use the PAI to identify your current SKAE. Compare your current SKAE against the SKAE required for the future aim point. Identify the gaps. These are the areas that you will use to develop strategies to make your goals achievable.

---

[9] This is a modification to the KSA (Knowledge, Skill, Ability) model commonly used in government agencies to describe job prerequisites. A good description can be found on the web at www.va.gov/jobs/hiring/apply/ksa.asp

It has been said that luck is the intersection between preparation and opportunity[10]. The dual purpose of good mentorship is to create opportunity where it did not previously exist, and to make sure that when the opportunity arises, the mentee is prepared for it. Creating the timeline and investing the time and energy to do a SKAE gap analysis serves both.

### Building A Bridge To The Future

The mentor's next task is to work with the mentee to define short and long-term goals to close the SKAE gaps over time. This is about taking deliberate action aligned with the desired end state. These short and long-term goals provide critical stepping-stones that the mentee will use to develop action plans addressing the specific SKAE gaps that exist at each critical decision point on the timeline. In this way, the mentee can develop incremental growth paths that draw the desired future closer with every major life decision.

This important step takes at least a couple of mentor sessions to allow sufficient time to review the gaps, prioritize them, and identify alternative ways to close them. Here the mentor's life experiences can play an important role as options and consequences are assessed in the context of the mentee's life. Try not to artificially limit the discussion on the front end by picking just one or two areas to examine. Make the conversations broad and rich. The focus remains on getting to that desired future with candor and authenticity.

With the deep knowledge provided by the PAI coupled with the timeline, the mentor can more purposefully guide the mentee through a richer analysis about each of the options, qualifications, life fit, and consequences of each future choice.

---

[10] Seneca, Roman dramatist, philosopher and politician (5 BC - 65 AD)

We will talk more about how to compare various courses of action in a subsequent chapter.

Timeline conversations can be very rich and empowering. By using a deliberate process to understand why previous life decisions were made, projecting forward to define a desired future, then leveraging SKAE gap analysis to create focused goals, the mentee can make any desired future possible. This is personal strategic planning at the basic level. Rather than being trapped by the past, the mentee can take responsibility for defining a different future, one targeted at his or her goals and aligned with their personal passion in life. It takes a lot of work to get to this point, but the work is noble and life giving. Ultimately it is worth every bit of effort, both for the mentee and the mentor.

## Step 4:  Developing Refined Personal Life Strategies

The work done to this point has set the stage for developing meaningful action plans that can incrementally move them in the direction of their desired future. As with any strategic plan, getting from point "A" to point "B" is not a direct path. There are always successes, failures and unknowns that impede progress and have to be considered in the plans.

### Selecting Focus Areas For Growth

It's easy at this stage for a mentee to feel overwhelmed with so much to think about and act upon. Through the SKAE analysis, the mentor can best support the mentee by helping narrow the initial focus to the top 2-3 areas where gaps exist. I call these "strategic thrusts" because they represent the high-payoff areas where personal effort can make a significant difference in the mentee's life. There is no right or wrong answer here so long as the mentor helps the mentee develop personal action plans that close the SKAE gaps and grow them toward their desired future.

Depending on the mentee's life goals, the gaps may involve education, self-improvement, physical health, life experiences, work experiences, spiritual development, volunteer work, or any activity that addresses SKAE gaps. I encourage my mentees to start small then expand as you make progress. Pick an area that needs growth, develop a plan to address the need, set a timeline with milestones for getting the work done, and hold yourself accountable. Adjust the action plans as life unfolds and circumstances change. Revisit your PAI and your vision, keep them current and make them "living" documents, relevant tools that you will continually use along the journey.

### Moving From Hope To Results

During this phase the mentor can best serve as a knowledgeable, invested coach, a sounding board to offer encouragement and perspective. By this time, the mentor and mentee will have established a close working relationship where candid feedback is expected, given and appreciated. This is the phase where much of the day-to-day workload shifts toward executing the action plans that turn hope into results. Follow-on mentor sessions should focus on tracking progress, creating disciplined accountability, and considering life changes that impact on the existing action plans.

This is also the stage where I typically connect the mentee to my personal network of professional contacts. By this time, the mentee's commitment to positive change is evident. The time is right to introduce them to a broader scale of personal mentor resources. Leveraging my network and expending social capital on behalf of the mentee creates opportunity space and broadens the mentee's base of support. New intersections can create new possibilities that can be of great help as the mentee executes their life strategies. We all know that it's not enough to just be good. Who knows that you are good is equally important, and that does not happen by accident. Sharing their network is one of the mentor's most important responsibilities. It is also one of the most valuable contributions that can be made to further a mentee's growth as they execute their life strategies.

## Step 5:  Executing the Discipline

### Mentoring is not something you do, it is something you become

A mentor's journey lasts a lifetime. As with any life skill, the more you mentor the more proficient and effective you will become at it and the more your Mentor Intelligence™ will grow. If you have made the decision to give this process a try, share that with your mentee. Let them know that you are a work in progress and that you will learn as they do. You will both benefit from doing that.

I have some mentees who get frustrated with life situations yet they have not invested the time and energy on the front end of the process. They will continue to be frustrated. Until a person comes to terms with the big questions of their life, the little ones are not going to make sense. This process loads the front end with that work and it provides context for everything else that happens. I constantly challenge the mentors I am training as well as my mentees to be patient, to resist the urge to jump right in and solve problems until they have built the foundation of a relationship and come to terms with the larger life questions.

Following a process, either this one or any other one that works for you, requires discipline for both the mentor and the mentee. The rewards operate on many levels. The mentee understands

75

that your goal as a mentor is not to tell them what to do but rather to help them gain control over their life decisions. That provides the mentee with life skills they can use throughout their life as well as pass on to future generations. They learn from your example that relationship is the underpinning of everything meaningful in life. They learn that any goal is achievable if the right amount of thought, planning and effort are put into it. They can also learn the life gift of giving something back through empowerment – giving a hand up rather than a hand out.

When life's crises pass and the mentee's immediate sense of urgency fades, give them a little nudge, call them up and ask them how things are going. Check in with them. Offer to set up additional mentee sessions. Sometimes, my mentees have been embarrassed by their own lack of progress on their journey, and in their embarrassment, let the sessions fade. This is where a gentle supportive nudge by a caring, non-judging mentor can make all the difference in the world.

I also recommend revisiting the PAI and personal development timeline at least once a year. Things change, and updating these tools keeps them relevant to the mentee and offers yet another indication that you are in this for the long haul. The more you invest in your mentees, the more they will respond in kind. They will repay your gift many times over with their own mentees because of your personal outreach and example. Simply taking the first step and committing to becoming a mentor is to teach by example, and there is no better way to begin.

### A Blueprint for Exploring Possibilities

(1) Building life strategies is the highest form of personal mentoring. It should be founded on the whole person

concept, understanding life's larger questions, deep self-awareness, and purposeful action toward personal vision.

(2) Strategic planning is a disciplined process that can help any person regardless of circumstance or position, creating meaningful life strategies.

(3) This section details a practical, five step sequential process any mentor can use to guide a mentee to reach their dreams. The steps are not difficult but have to be used to gain proficiency. As with anything of value in life, achieving life strategies requires thought, effort, discipline, and committed action to move from hope to reality.

(4) I have provided two powerful tools, the Personal Asset Inventory (PAI) and the Personal Development Timeline, to help the mentee move from self-awareness to developing purposeful strategic plans for their life. Using these tools in a structured approach puts the mentee on the path to fulfillment in a deliberate way, creates opportunity space, and increases the mentee's life skills.

(5) The mentor plays a critical role in this phase guiding and supporting the mentee through each phase of the process. Both mentor and mentee will benefit from the insights gained in each step.

(6) Perhaps the greatest gift a mentor can give is to share network and social capital with the mentee. This advocacy can be life changing.

*Chapter Five Practical Exercise*
*Questions For Personal Reflection and Growth*

1. Have you ever taken the Myers-Briggs Type Indicator ® or any other personality instrument? What is your personality profile? How do your preferences impact on others? How self-aware do you consider yourself?

2. Have you ever built a strengths-weaknesses chart? What is your personal "brand"? Do you think others see you the way that you see yourself? How do you know?

3. Where do you want to be in 20-30 years? Why are you on this earth and what is your life's purpose? How will you define richness and success in life?

4. Have you ever built a personal development timeline to visualize your life's decisions and vision for the future? When you compare your skills, knowledge, attributes and experiences (SKAE) today with your assessment of what you will need to achieve your dreams, where are the largest gaps and how are you going to close them?

5. Do you have a personal strategy? If so, how are you making it real in your life? Do you have a structured approach for personal growth? Are you shaping your future or being shaped by your future?

7. If you are a mentor, have you ever helped your mentee develop life strategies? How did you do it? How do you help them make incremental progress toward their dreams?

# Chapter Six: Tools To Empower Mentor Relationships

As you develop your skills as true partners in mentor relationships, you will be able to help each other achieve life goals as you navigate life's difficult decisions. This is not just about mentors supporting their mentees in traditional mentor relationships. The tools and techniques offered in this chapter can be used in <u>any</u> mutually beneficial mentoring relationship, or even by individuals who are simply looking for personal growth. Understanding human potential and supporting each other's journey by increasing decision making-skills is noble and fulfilling work.

### *Tool One: A Three-Dimensional View of Human Potential*

The first of these is a ***Talent Cube©*** (Figure 6.1), a simple visualization tool that offers a more complete view of talent. I developed the cube in response to my perception that leaders were often selected for advancement based primarily on their technical skills. As important as those skills are to being successful as an organizational leader, they are not sufficient to assess true potential. The cube presents the other dimensions of talent that I believe to be as important to life and leadership.

Each panel of the cube represents a different aspect of talent important to any leader position. The panels of the cube are dashed in the illustration to indicate that growth potential exists for every person in each dimension. This is an organic view of human capital and it is a really nice way to illustrate the other aspects of talent that can bring value to any organization or team.

By considering a person's character, leadership ability, passion, creativity, capacity and emotional intelligence in addition to technical skills, we can form a more complete view of any person's talent and set the stage for focused personal growth.

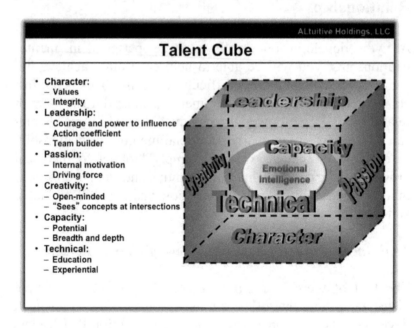

Figure 6.1 Talent Cube©

The cube can help anyone involved in a mentor relationship focus energy on those areas where growth is needed. As

Figure 6.2 illustrates, the essence of good mentorship is developing the talent of each partner to his or her full potential. By augmenting the PAI and SKAE analyses from previous mentor sessions, the cube can be used to visualize the greatest opportunities for personal growth.

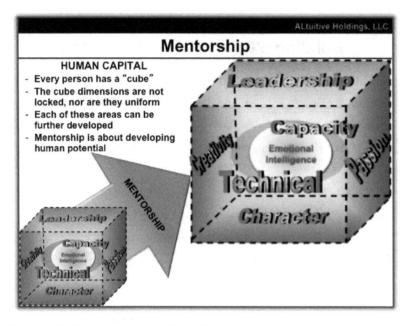

Figure 6.2 Mentorship and the Talent Cube

## *Tool Two: Navigating Life's Tough Decisions*

I think we all struggle with this area. Confronted with complex, tough decisions with multiple options and no simple answer, it is easy for anyone to get overwhelmed. Without some basic process to work through these options, there is nothing left but "gut" instinct, and that typically is not very effective. There is a better, more efficient and productive way to choose between life's options.

The tool I offer makes decision making much easier. It is a modification of a staff process used in the US Army Military Decision Making Process (MDMP) called the Course of Action (COA) analysis.[11] Once learned, it puts you squarely in the driver's seat of life's critical decisions and becomes hugely empowering.

## Building a Course of Action Matrix

- Step 1: Define the problem to be solved
- Step 2: Define Evaluation Criteria (EC) that you will use to compare each possible option
- Step 3: Identify the alternative solutions called Courses of Action (COA)
- Step 4: Build the matrix
- Step 5: Analyze each COA against each of the Evaluation Criteria (EC); assign numerical values across the matrix
- Step 6: Compare advantages and disadvantages
- Step 7: Pick the best option

Figure 6.3 Building a COA Matrix.

Figure 6.3 shows the seven steps in the process. While these steps are not complicated, they must be followed carefully and practiced to gain proficiency. The more time and energy you apply to this process the more effective your results will be.

---

[11] US Army, *Field Manual 5-0 Army Planning and Orders Production* (Washington, D.C.: HQDA), 20 January 2005. See Chapter 3 The Military Decision Making Process for a full description.

## *"What Swamp Are We Here To Drain?"*

**Step 1: Define the problem**. I once had a boss who would begin most of his meetings with the quote above. It was a folksy way of getting the group to define and focus on the real problem at hand. Rather than assuming that everyone was on the same sheet of music, he understood that the first step toward solving any problem was defining it in a way that everyone could see and understand. That was good advice then and it's good advice today.

Many times, the problem a mentee brings to me is not the real problem, but rather, a symptom of a larger problem they have not acknowledged or resolved. If we focus on the wrong problem, we will waste precious resources and not get closer to an effective solution. It takes Mentor Intelligence™ to ask the mentee the right questions, to listen to the responses, and to discern whether a larger life question underlies the perceived challenge. It bears repeating that until you come to grips with the larger questions of your life (like who are you and why you are here, what your unique gifts are and where your passion lies), the little questions (like where you work and what job you should take) won't make much sense.

## *How To Measure The Goodness Of Each Solution*

**Step 2: Define Evaluation Criteria (EC)**. Once the problem is defined, the next step is to identify the ***factors most important to you*** in evaluating the relative goodness of each of your choices. These factors are your Evaluation Criteria. They will help you identify the advantages and disadvantages as we review each alternative solution to find the best possible decision given the current circumstances. That is the process in a nutshell.

To visualize the process and show how these pieces fit together, I am going to use a simple notional example that closely replicates what I have encountered in mentoring. Let's consider a situation where a mentee has an opportunity to move to a new, higher paying job in the same location but with a different company. The problem statement is simply *"Do I take the new job or not?"*

In this example, let's assume the mentee has a bachelor's degree, is newly married, and joined a large company as an entry-level employee. All these factors impact on the decision and its outcomes. As is usually the case, there is no single or simple answer, only choices with consequences to consider.

The mentee contacts me and we set up a session to consider the problem and to evaluate his choices. Since we have already defined our problem statement, the next step is to identify the factors that are most important to him at this time. We determine that minimizing risk, increasing compensation, finding true growth potential, maintaining a good quality of life and staying in the location are the things that he values the most at this stage of his life and career. These are the EC we will use to evaluate the alternative COAs.

Developing EC is not always as simple in real life as it is in this example. If you are struggling with important life decisions, I encourage you to start now – write down the factors that are most important in your life. Use loved ones and mentors as sounding boards. When one of my mentor partners is struggling with a decision where there are multiple approaches, I often begin by asking them to take the time to sit in a quiet place and to write down the top 5-10 things that are most important in their life. In the ensuing dialogue, it is not hard to hone that list down to the top factors that are most important in evaluating each competing COA. Once you have them written down do your best to put them in priority order.

Chances are some will be more important than others – this is important because we will list them in priority order on the matrix.

Learning how to develop meaningful EC is an art form that takes a lot of self-awareness and reflection. Because it is so critical to making informed life decisions, it really is the magic ingredient in this process. It has the power to simplify very complex, multi-dimensional problems and point you to the best solution set. It also has intrinsic value in helping you discuss alternative solutions with your loved ones.

For this and each remaining step, once complete, cycle back to the first step – "Define the Problem" – and do a sanity check to make sure you stay connected to the real problem!

**Step 3: Identify Alternative Courses of Action (COA).** For most life challenges there are usually many different ways to address the problem. Frequently the real challenge is that there is no apparent simple answer to the more complex challenges we face, only alternatives, each having unique advantages and disadvantages that need to be considered. The role of the mentor at this step is to make sure that the mentee has identified *all viable options* without prematurely rejecting one or more before the analysis has been completed. This step is also helpful in reminding the mentee that he or she is in control of the situation and will make the ultimate decision about how to respond to the challenge rather than simply react to what someone else does to them. In this way, identifying COA can be very empowering. For our simple notional example, three alternative COAs will be considered: (1) take the new job, (2) stay in the old job, or (3) consider a completely out of the box idea like going back to school.

**Step 4: Build the Matrix**. At this point in our notional example, we have a problem statement, three COA, and five EC. We have everything that we need to build a COA matrix. Down the left side of a single sheet of paper we list the EC in priority order (↓). Across the top (→) we list each COA. I usually give them short one or two word identifiers such as "status quo", "new job", or "school" for simplicity. Figure 6.4 below is our notional COA matrix that we will use to analyze our three alternative COAs. It is a very simple comparison table. After laying out the EC and COA, our next step is to fill in the values.

ALtuitive Holdings, LLC

## Notional Course of Action (COA) Matrix

| COURSE OF ACTION / EVALUATION CRITERIA | Status Quo | New Job | School |
|---|---|---|---|
| Risk | 1 | 2 | 3 |
| Compensation | 2 | 1 | 3 |
| Growth Potential | 3 | 2 | 1 |
| Quality of Life | 1 | 3 | 2 |
| Location | 1 | 1 | 3 |
| **TOTAL** | 8 | 9 | 12 |

Figure 6.4 Notional COA Matrix for Example Problem Statement: "Do I take the new job or not"

**Step 5: Analyze each COA against each EC**. We are going to analyze each COA against each EC by assigning numerical values in each space on the matrix based on which COA is best for that particular factor. You can pick any scale that you want, but I always give the lowest number to the <u>best</u> COA measured against any EC and the <u>highest</u> number to the worst COA. It's easy for me to remember that #1 is best; since lower is better, the lowest total will identify the best COA, at least as measured against the selected evaluation criteria.

Let me walk you through this example matrix. Our first EC for comparison is "Risk." In this situation, the "Status Quo" COA (holding on to the current job) is the lowest risk and therefore the best COA against this EC so we give it a value of "1".

Quitting work to go back to school is the highest risk and therefore the worst COA against this EC so we give it a value of "3". Taking the new job is the second riskiest option so it gets a value of "2."

We repeat this process for each of the remaining EC. Although this can be done by the mentee alone, I strongly advise doing it as a team – mentor and mentee, or mentor partners. The back-and-forth dialogue is useful. It also helps the mentor understand why the mentee feels a certain way about the options and measures of effectiveness ratings.

For illustration purposes only, I have filled out the rest of the matrix assigning the "new job" option as the best COA for compensation (it is higher paying), "going back to school" as the best COA for future potential (increases qualifications), the "status quo" as the best COA for quality of life (it is the least disruptive) and "status quo" and "new job" as a tie for location (they are both in the same place). I identified what I thought to be the second best and worst option for each EC and assigned the values you see in the matrix.

### *The Bottom Line*

**Step 6: Compare advantages and disadvantages**. Now it's time to consider the results of the analysis by checking out the totals at the bottom of the matrix. Remember that the lowest total is the best option; the highest total is the worst option. In this example, the status quo (the current job) is actually best against these five measures of effectiveness, but not by much. Taking the new job is only one point off. Because these two COA are so close, I would have further conversations with the mentee to see if there were other factors (new EC) that we should have considered. Many times, this first pass at the matrix helps the mentee identify other factors that should be included in the analysis. It is also very common that one or more of the EC are so critical to the decision that it needs to be weighted in comparison to the other EC. In these cases, simply multiply the value of the EC by the desired factor. If the EC is twice as important as the other factors, the scale becomes 2,4, and 6 rather than 1,2 and 3.

With the matrix complete, it's time to assess each COA. Write down the advantages and disadvantages of each option based on the values assigned and talk them through with your mentor partner. There is seldom a perfect answer – every COA will have plusses and minuses that have to be considered. This methodical approach makes those advantages and disadvantages crystal clear and gives the mentee a visual representation to share with others. The visualization alone is worth the effort.

*Choose Wisely*

**Step 7:** **Pick the best option**. After advantages and disadvantages are reviewed, it's time to make a decision. Sometimes my mentees want to consider a hybrid COA – one that is a blend of the others, or perhaps even a completely different one that came up in the process. This is a perfectly acceptable outcome. By taking the time to understand each COA against a high-value set of EC, the mentee is much more likely to make an informed decision based on logic and analysis, not just "gut."

Through this process, the mentee is also better prepared to monitor impacts and outcomes as the decision is executed, adjusting the decision if needed as the facts surrounding the problem become clearer over time. New options and new possibilities emerge as the fruits of this effort, empowering the mentee to retain ultimate control of the situation rather than being victimized by any circumstance.

*What's In Your Life's Tool Box?*

Throughout this book I have provided practical tools that can be used to sort through tough challenges at home or at work. All of them have been used in my mentor practice and they work. My hope is that mentors and mentees alike will take these tools, learn them, apply them in their own journeys, and take them to the next level! For anyone seeking more effective mentor relationships, these tools can reduce the complexity and frustration we all struggle with from time to time, and teach valuable life skills in the process.

*A Blueprint for Exploring Possibilities*

(1) One of a mentor's greatest responsibilities is developing and maximizing each mentee's potential. Often,

organizations and leaders take a very narrow, limited view of talent that minimizes rather than maximizes human potential. The Talent Cube is a more holistic, organic way to considering talent in multiple dimensions: character, leadership, passion, creativity, capacity, and technical skills, all surrounding a core of emotional intelligence. This tool can be of great value in mentor relationships to identify areas for personal growth and expand the potential of every person.

(2) Helping mentees work through critical, complex life decisions is one of the most important and rewarding mentor responsibilities. It's important to resist the temptation to offer solutions that no mentor has to live with. Instead, I teach my mentees a process they can use themselves to visualize problems and evaluate alternative solutions more completely. By following the seven steps I outlined for this process, my mentees gain a life skill that can support them through their most difficult challenges. Equally important, the process makes the decision-making process visible, a great benefit to those most affected by the mentee's decisions.

(3) As with anything good in life, the more you use these tools, the more proficient you will become with them, and the more effective you will be as a mentor and as a mentee. Make the investment and it will reward you and your relationships, both at work and at home.

*Chapter Six Practical Exercise*
*Questions For Personal Reflection and Growth*


1.  When you think about human potential, both in yourself and in others, what characteristics do you consider important? When you viewed the Talent Cube©, what was your immediate reaction? If you are a hiring manager, when you have an open position, do you write the job requisition to include all these dimensions? If not which ones do you think should be ignored?

2.  When you are struggling with complex and important life issues with multiple options, do you use a structured process to sort through the options? Have you ever made a significant bad decision because you failed to consider something important? When you are working through your issues how do you make your thought processes visible to your loved ones?

3.  If you are a mentor, what process do you use to guide your mentee through tough situations? Have you ever used a tool like the COA Matrix? How effective was it at helping the mentee understand alternatives and consequences?

# Chapter Seven: Mentoring From The Heart

What have I learned on this life journey? Mentoring has been so full of teaching moments that have enriched my life beyond reason. I share them with you in the hope that you find them in your heart as well as you grow your own Mentor Intelligence™ and change others' lives in the process.

### The Power of Two$^E$

As I began to write this book, I reflected on the increasing isolation that seems to affect all of us in one way or the other. Isolation can grip a person's soul and suck the life out of them. Feeling alone and secluded, these people, each a special and unique creation of God, can act out in unimaginable and destructive ways.

It does not have to be this way. We have a choice, each of us, to ignore the separation around us or to connect and create an alternative path of hope and promise rather than anger, pain and destruction. Our young people need a hand-up today, not a hand out. They need us to connect with them at the life level, talk to them like they are real people with good minds and capable hearts, and give them a human connection to counter the loneliness and isolation so many of them feel. This is what mentorship is all about; it's what I call "The Power of Two."

I gained.this enabling insight from a very special mentor who has taken my life and my thoughts about mentorship to the next level. His name is Tom Tuohy. Tom is the founder of a non-profit organization called Dreams for Kids (DFK).[12]  This organization teaches at risk youth career and life skills as they build social enterprises to make the world a better place. DFK turns the world of isolation and loneliness for disadvantaged youth upside down. As they learn and grow, they move from being the problem to being the solution. This changes the world one kid at a time.

Tom's personal example of the "Power of Two" is about taking one extraordinary step to reach out to another human being without expectation or judgment to give their life new meaning and purpose. It is about teaching someone to rise above circumstance, disadvantage, adversity, or disability and creating new possibility in another person's life. It is about owning a future created by deliberate personal example. It is about living a life of significance through mentorship. It is also the finest example of organizational mentorship that I know encompassing Tom, his staff, his board of directors, and his army of volunteers.

Each of us has the opportunity to live the "Power of Two" every day. Reach out to someone else today, take a chance, take the risk, make a real connection and find the meaning of significance in your own life. No one should ever be alone so long as another of us has breath. This is the highest form of mentoring.

---

[12] See www.dreamsforkids.org

By combining our talents, our skills and our personal efforts, we can take the power of two to the next level and create critical mass – that is what "The Power of Two$^E$" represents as our efforts converge and combine to change our world for the better.

### Life-Changing Reverse Mentorship

In my earlier mentoring years, I focused more on offering my mentees the benefit of my wisdom rather than on discerning the wisdom I might be able to gain from them. Of course that was about ego. As I grew as a mentor and a leader, I began to understand that I was turning my back on a valuable life resource. Opening my ears (and my heart) to what I might learn from my mentees has provided me with some of my life's richest insights. Most importantly it has taught me that the most effective mentoring is about listening more than talking, something very difficult for a raging extrovert like me to master!

This book is evidence of the impact that insight has had on my life. As with any other life skill, the more I practiced the discipline, the better I got at it, and the richer the lessons became. Reverse mentoring is about learning from your mentees and creating mutually supportive relationships in the process. While your mentees may not have your years of experience, they bring their own unique experiences, perspectives and insights that can be of great value in your life if you give them a voice. Three wonderful examples follow.

The first of these insights came from a member of a mentee group I created (ELSWG) discussed later in this section. Our group was discussing work-life balance, a very important topic for all of us. This person shared a story about how his efforts to achieve work-life balance had not worked. He became so absorbed with the stresses of his work life that he became seriously ill. He made a comment that changed my life and that of the other group members when he explained that words matter, and that because of his personal experience, he knew that the phrase needed to change from "work-life balance" to "life-work balance." What an incredible and powerful insight, especially for emerging leaders. Even the way we typically choose to talk about finding the balance starts with work rather than life! Though that elusive balance between life and work necessarily shifts as we gain new and increased responsibilities, this is still a valuable perspective. For new leaders migrating from being individual contributors to leading teams, it is especially important to understand that your new responsibilities to the team will impact your own balance as you learn how to lead. Finding a proper balance and setting a good example for the other members of your team will take time, but pay great dividends. For mentors helping their mentees manage leadership transitions, keeping the "life" part of "life-work" balance at the forefront sets the stage for a lifetime of decision-making.

The same group gave me a second great example of reverse mentorship. Our group would share books of significance about various topics, and one of these books was "*Super Immunity*" by Joel Fuhrman.[13] A number of weeks after the group discussion, one of the group members followed me to my office and asked me if I had read the book. I had not, and she challenged me to make the time to read it and learn. She was holding me accountable for learning as much as I held the mentee group accountable for learning. I heeded her advice.

Through insights from the book and support from my family, I began to understand more fully the critical connection between health and nutrition. I even started a blog on a healthy lifestyles website so I could share my health journey with

---

[13] Joel Fuhrman, M.D., *Super Immunity* (Harper Collins: New York) 2011.

others.[14] Reverse mentoring has the power to change the life of the mentor just as the mentor hopes to change the life of the mentee.

My third and most personal example of reverse mentoring involves my diversity and inclusion (D/I) journey. I have always prided myself on being an "inclusive" leader, but over the last few years I learned that my inclusiveness had limits that I needed to admit and address. I had come a long way on my diversity journey when it came to race, culture, religion, socio-economic status, age and gender. My issue was sexual orientation.

The GLBTA (Gays, Lesbians, Bisexual, Transgender and Allies) community was a community I did not understand. More importantly, I did not want to understand it. Twenty-six years of "don't ask, don't tell" in the military had socialized me to believe that there was something different and wrong with members of that community. Frankly, I was more challenged with the concept of gay men and transgender people than I was with lesbians and bisexuals. But even with them, my approach was simply to avoid and ignore them all. The less I knew, the better off I was. At least that's what I thought at the time.

The corporation that I worked for had an authentic diversity/inclusion (D/I) program supported at the very top of the company's leadership. Through the great work they did with diversity training, I was given the opportunity to face into my own insecurities. I was designated a D/I "Game Changer" and was able to attend conferences designed to help me on my journey. At one of those conferences, the final speaker pitched a slide that said "What Are You Afraid Of" and he talked about running toward our differences rather than running away from them.[15] I started reflecting on the connection between

---

[14] The website is www.cheapchicorganic.com . I blog as "Frydaddy."

leadership and diversity/inclusion and knew in my heart that I had to change if I wanted to grow as a leader.

That insight changed me forever. I started to examine my own life and what I was running away from. I knew that as an organizational leader I had as great a responsibility to the members of the GLBTA community as I had to everyone else, no exceptions. I acknowledged that I had a long way to go on my journey to truly accept everyone in the work place regardless of sexual orientation, and I committed to work at it. I asked individuals from the GLBTA community to become my diversity partners to help me grow on this journey, and they accepted.

Through their reverse mentoring, I became a visible straight ally to the GLBTA community at work. I exposed myself to their concerns and frustrations in the work place. I let myself be open to the pain and isolation most of them have throughout their lives from rejection, judgment and fear of others. Most important of all, I let myself be open to their generosity and their friendship. Finally, after two years of wrestling with the question, I attended the 2011 "Out and Equal" Conference[16] and I learned as much about myself as I learned about the GLBTA community.

I left that conference determined to be a responsible leader, to stand up and be counted as an ally. This meant action not talk, and it was up to me to create a safe work place environment for members of the GLBTA community where they could bring their whole selves to work every day without fear, rejection or prejudice. I know this can be a charged issue, so I ask one simple question to those who share the struggle I just described: Who would you deny that right to?

---

[15] Reggie Butler, Raytheon Diversity Summit, Denver, Colorado 2008.

[16] Out and Equal Conference, Dallas, Texas, November 2011

This is a lifelong journey, but now I have new companions to help me grow along the way. My life has been so enriched by their friendship, and I have become a better leader and a better person because of their investment in me. This is the essence of reverse mentorship. It is a gift, but it only comes when the mentor's mind and heart are open for learning. Seek, and you will indeed find.[17]

### *Making Time For What Is Most Important*

During my years as a corporate business development director, I had a fairly packed daily schedule with early mornings, late evenings and lots of meetings in between. Over time I developed a workplace routine that was a combination of things I was required to do (such as attend meetings) along with things every leader should do (such as mentoring). Almost every leader I knew developed a similar routine.

As you progress up the corporate ladder, it is increasingly difficult to carve out time for activities such as mentoring which are often viewed as optional. I want to reinforce a point that I have made repeatedly in this book – mentoring is a personal choice. The best leaders that I have met treat mentoring the same as the "required-to-do" activities. These leaders do not require anyone to make mentoring sessions mandatory. They understand that it is a basic leader responsibility to grow the business by growing the next generation of leaders. They make the time in their routine, no matter how busy they are or how high they climb in the organization, to make mentoring happen.

At a recent presentation I gave to a large group about mentoring, one of the senior leaders made the comment that

---

[17] Matthew 7:7-8

she was too busy to pick up additional mentees. Even with good mentors, that is a commonly shared perspective. The problem is that this is exactly what everyone else in the room is thinking. You can almost read their minds: "I am already swamped and the last thing I can afford to do is to take on more responsibility!" Yet that is exactly what needs to happen to rise to the need.

Rather than viewing this from the perspective of your time, let's consider it from the perspective of need. Look around the organizations you belong to. How are things going? What is the mood of your team? Are employees feeling more or less secure about their jobs and their careers? When you make the time to talk with the newest employees, what do they tell you about the climate of the organization? Let the need define your actions rather than time.

We can always find excuses or say we are already doing enough. Said enough times, it may even sound convincing, at least in our own minds. Yet when we look at it objectively, that will only sustain the status quo in our organizations. If nothing changes, nothing changes!

Sometimes I think we have our priorities backwards. We tend to treat those daily and weekly organizational meetings as so important that we can't miss them. Amazingly, if we do miss one, the world does not come to an end. I am not suggesting that leaders skip the inevitable corporate meetings (as attractive as that may be!). I am only suggesting that we should all consider missing a mentor/mentee session as more important because it may have greater consequence. It should be treated with the same intentional support and deliberate action as those "have-to-do" things that are more visible to our bosses.

Make the time to mentor, make it part of your routine whatever that routine is, and know that at the end of every day, what you do here will matter far more than what happens at most required organizational meetings. At the end of the day, people grow the business, not meetings and not machines. The more we all invest in the development of our teams, the more they will deliver for us and for our organizations. The competitive advantage of any organization rests with its people – enough said!

### *Group Mentoring - The Magic of ELSWG*

Several years ago I took part in a number of Large Group Interactive (LGI) dialogues, events where senior organizational leaders would meet with several (>100) early career employees to have candid dialogue about our business. These were wonderful sessions chock full of insights and opportunities. Through them I became sensitized to a mentoring gap that existed in some of our teams and I wanted to do something about it.

As it seems with most of life's significant challenges, you are either part of the problem or part of the solution. While I was already active as a mentor I did not feel that I was doing enough. After a lot of reflection I came to the realization that mentoring did not have to be a one-on-one activity. From that insight I began what became one of the most rewarding experiences in my life!

I recruited a young engineer in our company to help me find ten or so early career employees. I wanted them to be a diverse group (i.e., not all white male engineers) and asked that each candidate be "acknowledged as a leader by their peers." Unlike the elitist leader programs I discussed earlier in the book, I wanted to include the kinds of emerging leaders often excluded by circumstance or visibility in these more formal programs. At the time I was serving as strategy director for our organization. My intent was to create a small group of early career leaders with whom I could share the strategy on a more personal and engaged level. I wanted to take some positive action to begin to close the gap that the LGI had made evident to me. I also wanted to help our business grow.

I prepared a brief presentation on my intent and shared it with my leadership, with the Human Resources (HR) VP, and with the Deputy General Manager of the business. With their support including some nominations from the HR VP, I created the group and called it the Junior Strategy Work Group (JSWG). That began a journey of discovery learning that continues to this day. I established 1 ½ hour monthly sessions where I provided lunch for the group. We would meet for dialogue, lively conversation, and mentoring. Over time our topics grew to include leadership, diversity and inclusion, difficult conversations, dealing with adversity, tough business decisions, personal life-work balance, health, and a host of other topics usually suggested by one of the attendees.

Within the first year the group pushed-back on the name JSWG commenting that they did not like to be called "junior" anything! Rather than assuming that I had the answer, we worked together to come up with a better name, and the Emerging Leader Strategy Work Group, or ELSWG was born.

Every month attendance would vary depending on individual schedules. Since members came from the breadth and depth of the organization, we never had the exact same group present, which only added to the richness. To expand our reach to those who could not attend each session and to offer ELSWG access beyond the meetings, we created an e-room where members could post material and review anything covered by the group during the meetings. The room became the team's repository for presentations on strategy, leadership philosophies and insights, team member MBTI® profiles and dealing with different personality types, group input on work challenges and difficult situations, dealing with adversity and turning it into advantage, book reviews, and other think pieces of value to the team.

Over time, and even with varied attendance, the sessions became deeper, more candid, and more insightful as the years passed and our relationships grew. As I had hoped, ELSWG became "mentorship glue" for the members, a place to have safe, authentic conversations about important topics, and most importantly, we created a unique network of emerging leaders with influence across the organization.

By July 2012, we had over 75 members in the e-room and our monthly attendance averaged between 27 and 30. Some, not all, of the members took the additional step of asking me to serve as a personal mentor for them as well, and those relationships continue to this day.

From this section, my hope is to inspire others to step out, to see the mentor vacuums where they exist, and to do something about it. Not only is group mentorship possible, it is also the most powerful forum for reverse mentorship that I have ever experienced. Mentorship can change a life – group mentorship can change many lives at a time including the life of the mentor.

### Seeing Is Believing: Virtual Mentorship

While technology has unquestionably contributed to our increasing isolation, it has also provided the opportunity to conduct mentor sessions across time and space. The mobility of our society almost guarantees that we will not spend our lives in one location. Unlike our parents and their parents who frequently lived and died where they were born, today's generations are more likely to experience living in more than one location, perhaps even in different countries.

Technology closes the gap for the tech savvy. When our boys (both active duty Captains in the US Army) were deployed to Iraq and Afghanistan, our family was able to maintain contact (and sanity) through personal video teleconferencing programs such as Skype and Face Time, which allowed us to see their faces at the same time that we talked. As a parent, I can tell you how important that was and what a difference it made to understand how they were really doing. Over the years, the same has been true of our children, their spouses and the eight wonderful grandchildren they have blessed us with. Cards and letters are fine, calls are better, and video teleconferencing is better than that!

In mentorship, the advantages and the impact are the same. When distance prevents face-to-face sessions, Google+, Facetime and Skype all provide meaningful alternatives. Although none of them has the same impact as physically being there, they are good enough to use in conducting mentor sessions. Today I have regularly scheduled mentor sessions using these meeting tools. I have even been able to "meet" mentees virtually for the first time over this medium. Since we are able to connect almost anywhere we go, this opens the door to regularizing mentor sessions even after your ability to do face-to-face sessions ends. Mentorship, even if virtual, can continue over a lifetime across time and space.

### *Lifelong Learning*

This is such a foundational principal of mentorship that I felt obligated to include it here. In my view, when inquiry stops in a person, that person gives up the privilege of being a mentor. If you stop learning how can you be credible asking anyone else to grow?

Over the years, I would occasionally hear someone make a statement about another person (usually regarding disruptive or rude behavior) that so and so "is just that way!" The loud and clear message is that nothing and no one is going to change that person. But the real message is that the person has stopped growing. What an awful thing to say about any other person, and yet I have heard it said about both young and more senior employees and team members.

Nobody should get off the hook of self-improvement so long as they are part of any organization or team. Be a hermit if you want, but if you are part of an organization, you need to grow, if only to learn how to be more effective as a leader, a communicator, a team mate, a partner or a colleague. My advice is two-fold: (1) avoid saying this about anyone else, ever! (2) if you do hear it, push back – make the statement that each person on the team has an obligation to themselves and to one another to learn and to grow.

If such behavior is allowed to continue without challenge, it sets a horrible precedent for the organization. It almost always plays out in destructive ways for the individual and for the team. It defines a classical "lose-lose" situation.

No one is perfect, but sustained bad behaviors create damaged relationships, hurt people on the team, and impact productivity and performance across the organization. Sustained continuous improvement and lifelong learning can maximize the human capital of any team. We can all be better. If you lead by example as a mentor you can create a culture of openness to change and lifelong learning that will extend far beyond the workplace. Share your own journey, be vulnerable to learning, and gain the respect of everyone else in your life.

## *Active Mutual Support*

I think it's basic human nature that each of us finds some people a real pain to be around and to deal with. The reverse is also true – no matter how carefully you work to cultivate a positive brand, there will always be others who frankly do not want to be around you either. Several years ago I was exposed to the concept of active mutual support.[18] At its core, active mutual support is about owning every relationship, good as well as bad, and investing time, talent and energy in the success of those you like as well as those you do not like. It is about <u>taking the lead</u> to repair relationships when they break. By shifting the focus of a relationship breakdown from the other person to yourself and owning the personal responsibility to invest in that person's success, you turn the world upside down. In mentoring, I use this concept to help my mentees improve their relationships with special emphasis on those where there is a clear or perceived fracture.

While developing the PAI discussed in Chapter Five, I ask each mentee to invite others who know them (including those who may not have a positive opinion about the mentee) to provide three short phrases or words that describe the mentee. We all have these people are in our lives. As in any relationship, if we want things to improve with that person, we can either wait for that person to reach out to us or we can take control of the situation and reach out to that person. It is always a choice.

Often, the mentee will not even know why another person has an issue with them because they have not had a conversation about it. By reaching out and asking that person to be part of

---

[18] More information on the concept of active mutual support can be found at www.arbinger.com

the mentee's self-awareness exercise, not only is the mentee taking positive action to resolve the fracture, but also, this simple act often changes the opinion of the person about the mentee. It can create the positive foundation from which both parties can grow through active mutual support. Demonstrating to a mentee how he or she can begin to repair broken or fractured relationships teaches them a powerful life skill that can be used whenever and wherever the need arises. Fractured relationships can be fixed as long as one side is willing to take the first step. Even if there is no response from the other party, this act is where the moral high ground lies.

### *Advocacy*

This word means a lot of different things to different people. In my mentoring practice, I use it to mean leveraging all my resources to advance the career growth of a mentee. Typically, advocacy involves making personal recommendations on behalf of the mentee when position openings occur, providing introductions of the mentee to senior leaders whom I respect, sharing my professional networks with the mentee, writing letters of recommendation where possible, setting up meetings with subject matter experts in fields of interest, preparing mentees for interviews, and any number of other requests that make my resources available to the mentee. At its most basic level, advocacy is about staking my reputation on the mentee by presenting them to my inner circle of professional contacts. Personal recommendations carry a lot of weight and can make the difference between selection and non-selection. Because of the gravity of providing personal advocacy, I am careful about what I offer, when I offer it, and to whom, not only to protect my reputation with my peers and supervisors, but also to protect my mentees by not diluting the value of the sharing.

Advocacy is not an entitlement for any mentee, nor is it an "event" that releases the mentor from follow-up. While it may typically begin with a simple introduction at a social event, that is just the beginning of the joint responsibility shared by the mentor and the mentee. When I make the decision to stake my reputation on a mentee, I become responsible for following up with my connections to get their perspectives on the mentee, and the mentee becomes responsible for following up on the initial connection. As with every other aspect of good mentoring, advocacy is an iterative process requiring deliberate action and solid follow through. Mentor Intelligence™ plays a crucial role in this process, so the more developed a mentor's skills become, the more adept and effective they become as advocates.

### Decision-Making Skills

With very few exceptions over the years, my mentees from various backgrounds, disciplines and skill sets have needed help with making critical life decisions. This should be a required high school/college class because the need is so universal, the skills are so easy to learn, and the positive benefits can last a lifetime.

You might assume that the early career stage mentees represent the biggest need. I have found the problem to be much more pervasive. Many senior employees who have spent decades in the work force simply never learned the skill set. Every person is eventually faced with critical life decisions that are complex, have multiple options for resolution, and involve both practical and emotional issues. Of all the recommendations in this book, none is more important for the mentor than mastering some process for critical decision-making. In the previous chapter I offered the COA Matrix for this purpose. This decision-making tool puts sanity, focus and objectivity as counter-balances to the emotional content and "gut check" that we all tend to rely on. It works. More importantly, it puts the mentee squarely in the driver's seat and it empowers the mentee to become more self-reliant as they master critical analysis.

### *Abundance Thinking vs. Scarcity Thinking*

There are two different types of people in this world; those who always see increased win-win possibilities in life for everyone (abundance thinking) and those who believe that the only way for one person to gain in life is for another person to lose (scarcity thinking). Steven Covey created this concept in his seminal work, "The Seven Habits of Highly Effective People."[19] It's important to note that abundance thinking is not about unrealistic optimism nor is scarcity thinking just about unbridled pessimism. Good leadership and good teams frankly need a healthy balance of both optimism and pessimism to create effective solutions. The nuance here is that leaders who embody abundance thinking are able to take the negatives in any situation and create positive outcomes.

Imagine the contrasting perspectives and results between a mentor who believes in, and routinely practices, abundance thinking as opposed to one who believes in and practices scarcity thinking. Scarcity thinkers typically create a world of winners and losers, and that is what they teach. To them, winning is more important than anything else, including relationship. In this worldview losers lose because they deserve to. It is both destructive and dangerous, especially to those who are most at-risk or disadvantaged – diversity and inclusion are certain casualties.

In any life situation, each of us has the power to create lose-lose outcomes (a typical output of scarcity thinking), win-lose outcomes (the actual goal of scarcity thinking), or win-win

---

[19] Steven Covey, *The Seven Habits of Highly Effective People* (New York: Simon and Schuster, 1989), 219-220.

outcomes (the real goal of abundance thinking). Of course, it is always more challenging to create those win-win outcomes. It takes more effort, more humility, more compassion, more empathy and more understanding. It also takes Mentor Intelligence™. It saves and nurtures relationships and creates future possibilities the scarcity thinkers cannot envision or achieve. Reflect on your life choices and commit to a mentorship practice based on abundance thinking.

Guiding a mentee to see possibility where they did not, relationship where they could not, and growth where they would not, is high art, and represents one of the highest forms of personal mentorship. Sometimes, it is as simple as asking a mentee to envision what that elusive win-win would look like – something no scarcity person would ever ask. If you can envision it you can make it happen.

It can also be a very humbling experience to watch a mentee grow to become a morally balanced, ethical and effective leader, able to turn adversity into advantage for others, not just for themselves. For any leader there are few things as challenging as learning how to take what seems to be a negative situation (such as a draw down or disciplining a team member) and navigating a solution set that strengthens the team rather than weakening it, even if it comes at the expense of individual members. Abundance thinking balances pragmatism, judgment, discernment and hope to create that solution set.

Abundance thinking is also about making room in your mentality and behavior for diversity and inclusion. Scarcity thinking at its core is about judging of others as "less worthy" and hence, less deserving. It is only in abundance thinking that we create a level playing field regardless of advantage or privilege. This is mentoring from the heart.

## *A Blueprint for Exploring Possibilities*

(1) Mentorship is a way of life. Living that life offers the possibility of unique perspectives and lessons that will not only change your mentees' lives, but also change yours as well.

(2) Ten special empowering insights are offered for your consideration and application. They have changed my life, increased my Mentor Intelligence™, and helped me change the lives of my mentees.

(3) The only way to experience these insights is to make them your own. Bring these ideas, perspectives and tools into your mentor practice. Each is powerful in its own right – in combination they are a formidable force for good in this world.

*Chapter Seven Practical Exercise*
*Questions For Personal Reflection and Growth*

1. As you consider your own experiences with mentorship, what special insights have you gained that have changed your life as well as that of your mentees? How did you gain those insights and how have you incorporated them into your actions at home and at work? Have you shared them with anyone?

2. As you read the ten insights in this chapter, which ones stood out to you as most important? Why? How can you make those insights real in your own life and in the lives of those you are mentoring?

3. Have you ever experienced the power of reverse mentoring? What did you learn and how did it change your life?

4. Do you believe that mentorship can become a way of life for you? What does mentoring from the heart mean to you and to the people who are important in your life? Are you willing to commit to this life-giving change?

## Chapter Eight: Leading For Life

How could I end this book with any other topic? Leadership is the glue that holds the threads of Mentor Intelligence™ together. Leadership and mentorship are intertwined. Good leaders are good mentors. In this final chapter we will consider some perspectives that will make you a better leader and a better mentor. They will also help you increase your Mentor Intelligence™ as you use, and share, what you learn.

### *Making the Impossible Possible*

It is easy to look like a hero when things are going well. Too frequently, leaders miss the point that anyone can make the possible happen. Real leadership is about making the impossible happen, creating opportunities and carving potential out of chaos and adversity. That is the domain of real, meaningful leadership. It is about what we do and how we act when things go wrong, when the chips are down, and when it seems that the world is crashing around us and our teams.

*Navigating the Rapids – Leadership Matters*

To build a true legacy of leadership, you have to learn how to navigate the rapids of life. The ideas in this section are food for that journey representing leadership lessons I have learned through successes and failures of my own, with the help of great leaders and mentors. They also represent the foundations of my mentorship practice.

A few years ago I was asked to give the keynote address for a "Leadership Matters" graduating class. "Leadership Matters" is a powerful program created by the senior Engineering leadership of the organization I worked for. It was born out of the notion that good leaders make the best business decisions, and that they can be grown within any type of organization. This was the best corporate leadership development program I had ever seen and I wanted to do it justice.

In the three months that I had to prepare for the graduation, I spent a lot of time thinking about the content and structure of the presentation. I had grown tired of rote solutions and endless lists of leader characteristics. Leadership can't be taught or learned from a checklist. It has to be developed in a way that honors the unique creation each of us represents with our own experiences, personalities, skills and talents.

I reflected on Betsy Holden's powerful comments about developing the right questions before attempting to provide any answers, and I knew that this would frame my presentation. Rather than offering these young graduates any answers about leadership, I chose instead to create a leadership ecosystem based on core questions I felt every leader should ask before making any decision affecting the life of another person. These would have to be questions that every person could embrace, be relevant to their own lives, and be used as a guide in navigating leadership situations.

## *A Personal Leadership Ecosystem*

Over the next several weeks, I developed an eight-question framework that could be applied to any and every possible leadership situation. That is the unique value of a questions-based approach where context is provided by each leader and each situation. If someone in my life had to make a critical decision about my future, I would hope and pray that they would consider these questions before making the final decision. The eight questions are presented below along with the clarifying questions I included in my presentation for Leadership Matters (chart is included at Appendix B). I encourage you to print the chart and put it on the wall at home or in your work place. Use it as a guide as you face leadership decisions for yourself or for others. Answer the questions candidly – it might change how you decide, and more importantly, what you decide.

Indeed leadership does matter. My sincere hope is that every leader reading this book will take the time to think about these questions and use them to guide your decision-making about your life and those you lead. Answer them candidly – it might change how you decide, and more importantly, what you decide.

### *Run To The Sound Of The Gunfire!*

### *Question 1: From what direction do you lead?*
- Up or down or lateral? Why? What is your motivation?
- From the front or from behind? Do you run to, or away from, the sound of the "gunfire?"

Each of us has experienced "leaders" who were more concerned about their bosses than their teams. It is more rare, but occasionally I have seen leaders who were just the opposite – they were so overly concerned about their teams that they were reckless with their leadership. Seldom mentioned is the impact of lateral considerations, how what you do on your team impacts surrounding teams. Taken to an extreme, that can lead to groupthink, or on the other end, to unhealthy competition. As you consider any leader situation, take the time to consider your motivations. Why are you doing what you are doing? Who will benefit? What is the impact in all three directions?

In the military, we used to have this saying about running to the sound of the gunfire. It is an analogy for leading from the front, having the courage to expose yourself to the same danger and risk that your team faces. Military history provides instructive examples such as the generals in World War I who ordered hundreds of thousands of soldiers to their deaths on the front lines from the safety of their chateaus.[20]

Cowardice is cowardice no matter how you dice it. When problems hit your team, how do you respond? Do you jump into the fray and take charge or sit back and send in your teammates? When you hear the sound of gunfire, will you engage yourself and be part of the solution or turn the problem (and the risk) over to them? Are you visible on the front lines or are you in your personal "chateau"?

---

[20] Correlli Barnett, The Swordbearers (Bloomington: The Indiana University Press), 1963

*Learning the Value of What You Do Not Know*

***Question 2: How do you inform your decisions?***
- Do you value what you do know more than what you don't know?
- Do you know the difference? How?
- How can you fill your life's blind spots?

As senior leaders move up in their organization's ranks, it often seems that they begin to value <u>what they know</u> far more than <u>what they do not know</u>. There are blind spots in every situation. The trappings of office to include admins and staffs can serve to block information from the leader – the higher the staff the greater the filter! This is not a slam against administrative assistants or staffs – they do what their leaders expect them to do. The very best leaders that I know understand that and are very careful about what they ask for.

Before making any critical decision the thoughtful leader will take a step back, assess what is known and how it is known, think about how reliable the information is, identify where the gaps are and why they exist, and determine action that can be taken to close them.

Two classic examples of this kind of leadership action are skip-echelon meetings and <u>unannounced</u> visits to unexpected locations within the organization. It is amazing what leaders can discover about themselves and about their organizations by breaking routine and being open to what they do not know. In every case, these actions will result in better decisions.

## Faces and Reflections

### Question 3: What do you reflect to your team?
- When they see your face or hear your voice? Do they see their qualities and potential or do they see their shortfalls?
- Do you really invest in diversity or do you invest in "sameness"? Do you run toward the differences or away from them?
- Do you lead by example - "Walk the Talk"?

This question is fascinating to me. I have often shared with my mentees that the only part of your body that you cannot see without a mirror is your face. Yet to the rest of the world, your face (closely coupled to the tone of your voice) is the mirror to your soul, and it speaks volumes about what you really feel. You may intend to send out an innocuous message to a loved one or someone on your team and you get a completely unintended negative or defensive reaction. I think this happens more often than we would like to admit.

The disconnection is not always in our word choices (although that's important too), it's in the facial expressions that we do not see and in our tone of voice. From the time we are babies, we learn how to read and respond to them. Regardless of what is being said, they convey intent. They can convey acceptance or rejection and they have the power to lift up or to destroy.

When you look at your team members, what do they see? Do they see the critic that focuses more on faults and limitations or do they see a caring leader who focuses on qualities and potential? These really are different but closely related features of the same idea. Every leader needs to develop his or her team, and that means acknowledging faults, problems and shortfalls. But that can be done in a destructive way or in a

117

constructive way, and the choice will be evident in your facial expressions and tone of voice.

There is also a very important implication to diversity and inclusion here. We all know leaders who are not inclusive, who only want to be around those most like them. When they get someone "different" on the team, their facial expressions will say a lot about their behavior and their willingness to be open to the differences or not, regardless of what they say.

This leads to the final point about walking the talk. These are the three most important words in any leader's life. If you speak about respect, diversity and inclusion, and openness as a leader, but your actions are not aligned with those words, you will not be credible to anyone. Walk the talk, be visible and let your actions speak to your character.

### *The Power of Humility*

***Question 4: How do you wield your power as a leader?***
- As a gift or an entitlement? What opens your heart, your mind and your soul?
- With humility or arrogance? How can you tell?
- Do you focus on good intent or good result? Why is that important?

At its most basic level, leadership is about exerting power over another person's life. That power can be intoxicating especially for the emerging leader experiencing it for the first time. I have observed leaders who wielded that power almost as if it were a God-given right, an entitlement because they view themselves as better than those they lead. This is not about self-confidence; at its core it's about arrogance and egocentric leadership. If such leaders succeed, it will almost always come on the backs of their people.

On the other hand, accepting that any leadership position is a gift and exercising power with deep personal humility can lead to an open heart, an open mind and an open soul. There is a quiet power that comes from shifting the focus of your leadership from yourself to your team. It makes others want to work for you because they believe in you and trust you to do the right thing for them and the team rather than doing what increases your influence the most. A humble leader never loses sight of the responsibility to nurture, develop and grow the team.

The question about intent vs. effect reflects years of hearing leaders excuse results on the basis of good intent. That is a cop out. Good intent on any leader's part is a given. Leadership is about generating _good results_ based on that good intent. How many times have you heard someone say "I did not intend for that to happen," or "that's not what I meant, you heard me wrong." The leader is responsible for whatever happens, intended or not. Good leaders are not satisfied until the desired good effect is achieved. When leaders focus as much on result as on intent, goodness results.

This applies to critical leader communications as much as it does to actions. If you have a message that you want to deliver, sending the message is just step one, yet that is often where things stop. Monitoring how that person or your team responds is step two, and adjusting the message, the medium or the tone is step three. Follow through is not micromanaging; it is a basic leader responsibility. The job is not over until the desired results are achieved. The burden is on the sender, not the receiver, the leader not the led.

## The Credit Game

**Question 5:  Where do you point for successes?  What about for failures?**
- To yourself?  To your team?  To others?
- Do you ever pass up an opportunity to showcase your team?
- How important is credit to you (really)?

One of the greatest leadership quotes came from President Harry Truman when he said, "It's amazing what you can accomplish if you do not care who gets the credit."[21]  Yet in today's highly charged, competitive workplace, credit does matter.  The important leader question is how you manage, share, and balance it. Teams, not individuals, win.  The most incredibly successful leaders I have known were masters at the art of giving credit to their teams.  There were two discernable results:  (1) those teams always did better than the other teams, and (2) the leaders of those teams were highly respected, admired and greatly valued by their subordinates.

Ambition has both a good side and a bad side.  On the good side, it can lead to the drive to accomplish positive things.  On the bad side, it can create credit hogs, leaders who always want to be in the spotlight shining with their latest success.  That is the kind of leader no one wants to work for.

## The Ripples We Create In Our Passing

**Question 6:  What do you leave in your wake?**
- Do you lift others, elevate them or diminish them?
- Have you inspired others to achieve unseen possibilities or demoralized them with their imperfection?

---

[21] Harry S. Truman quotes (American 33rd President of the United States, 1884-1972)

- Can you see more in others than they see in themselves (and in yourself!) and provide opportunity for them to grow?

Imagine that you are floating on a boat in a lake. Behind you are all the people that you have encountered in your life since you got up this morning – your family members, the people in their cars on the highway, the people you walked past in the parking lot at work, the admins at the front desk who greeted you, the colleagues you passed in the hall at work, the people on your team - each of them in their own boats. What kind of ripples did you create in their lives today with your passing? Did you create ripples that upset them or did you help them on their own journeys?

I love this visualization because I think it reflects what really happens every day in each of our lives. We pass others and they pass us, and in the passing, we create opportunities to make a positive or a negative difference. Simple acts of kindness and compassion, doing something nice for another person and calling them by their name, the smallest of acts can create ripples that lift another person up. The life-giving power of actions like this for both the leader and the led can be understood more fully by reading *Resonant Leadership* by Richard E. Boyatzis and Annie McKee.[22]

As a leader you have the power to create positive ripples in the lives of your team members every day. Without expecting anything in return, you can empower them to grow beyond even what they see in themselves. Instead of focusing on their shortfalls and inadequacies, you can choose to focus on their gifts and their strengths. You can provide opportunity beyond their wildest dreams and make those dreams real. At the end of

---

[22] Richard Boyatzis and Annie McKee, *Resonant Leadership* (Boston: Harvard Business School Press, 2005)

the day, this will be your true legacy. It will not be in what you accomplished, but in what you left behind in the lives of those you led.

### *"There Are No Atheists In Foxholes"*

### *Question 7:  What is the source of your personal funding?*
- Can you answer the larger questions in your own life? Is your centering in self or something larger than self?
- How do you "add to your account"?
- What are your life debits and how do you pay them?

While there is considerable confusion about who first said "There are no atheists in foxholes,"[23] there is no doubt about its meaning. This is not about religion; it is about believing in a higher life source that frames the answers to the larger questions in your own life. Leadership is a battlefield, complex and full of risk to both the leader and the led. I believe that self-centered leadership is toxic. I also believe there is a connection between humility and believing in a higher life source. Leaders who believe they have all the answers to life's challenges within themselves are bound to eventually stumble on a situation that defies their best efforts. As they fall they take their teams with them.

Whatever your source of spiritual funding, acknowledging it as a centerpiece in your life will help you become a better, more caring, and ultimately more effective leader.

---

[23] "There are no atheists in foxholes" in *Wikipedia: The Free Encyclopedia*; (Wikipedia Foundation Inc., updated 4 April 2013, 5:52 UTC

**Question 8:** *When you are gone, what will be left behind, and will it really matter?*
- Are you living a life of self-importance or a life of significance?
- What does the final balance in your life's savings account say about your investments in others?

There are a lot of very successful people in this world who are terribly unhappy. For many of these leaders, the rise to the top came at the expense of everything else important in their lives. This is the true cost of self-importance. If that is what you seek, that is what you will end your life with, nothing but yourself.

Recently I reflected on the life of my grandfather. He lived to be 91 years old. When he died, this poor dirt farmer in east Texas was the richest man I ever knew because of all the people in his life who loved and respected him. He invested in what was truly most important in life – other people – and was richly rewarded to the end of his days. He did not have position or title or physical wealth. He just lived a humble life of significance creating the most incredible life savings account I've ever seen.

When you are gone, who will care? After all your promotions and raises and successes and accomplishments fade, what will be left? How will it define your life on this earth? Will it matter or will it evaporate the minute you pass? If you invest in others, there is no greater return for any life investment. To put this in perspective, my Army Chaplain friend Tim Bedsole once said that on their deathbed, he never saw any person ask for a promotion, title, position or pay raise. Without exception, he said that every person asked for three things – relationship with themself, relationship with their God (defined any way you like), and relationship with their family and friends. At the end of the day, that is the true definition of a life of significance.

## *A Blueprint for Exploring Possibilities*

(1) Personal leadership is the glue that ties everything important in life together. Leadership and mentorship are intertwined. Mentoring leadership is about creating opportunity space for each mentee and creating life-giving possibilities that would not be possible without mentor help.

(2) Navigating the "rapids" of life is challenging for everyone. We all need the help of a guide on that journey. Leadership decisions are a huge part of that journey impacting the lives of the leader as well as the led.

(3) This chapter presents a leader decision-making ecosystem. Rather than providing answers that have limited relevance, I offer instead the eight most critical questions that I think should frame every leader decision. Thinking through each of these questions will result in better decisions and will also grow the leader toward a life of significance, creating real legacy and growing Mentor Intelligence™ in the process.

*Chapter Eight Practical Exercise*
*Questions For Personal Reflection and Growth*

1.  Using your own life experiences as a guide, what do you think the connection is between leadership and mentoring?

2.  What do you use as a guide to help you make the best leader decisions possible in your work life and your personal life? How did you feel reading the eight questions in the ecosystem? Did the questions resonate with you? Are there others that you think you should consider every time you have to make a decision that affects others?

3.  As you reflect on your work experiences, how can you find a greater balance between self-importance and significance in your life and in the life of those you influence? How do you define richness in life? When you are gone, how do you want to be remembered and what will you do to create that legacy?

## Chapter Nine: Taking Flight

As I considered various titles for the book, I settled on calling it a field guide because that captured the most valuable use of these insights, perspectives and tools. The most important question I would ask each of you is what are you going to do with this knowledge? Mentor Intelligence™ has the power to change the world, one life at a time. Imagine a world where it became as important as the other forms of intelligence that we use to identify ourselves as mature adults, a world where we each create a vibrant legacy of deep, lasting relationship that spans generations. With your help, we can make that dream real.

The value of a field guide is that it can be pulled out from time to time, most especially when we seek ideas or answers to specific questions as they come up. Put this book to use in your homes, your places of work, and your social organizations. Actively seek others who might benefit from your own journey toward Mentor Intelligence™ and take that first step toward creating more meaningful and valuable relationships, either as a mentor, a mentee, or simply a mentor partner. Link arms and form a community of interest wherever you are in your own life. Put these tools to use, develop your own, and add to the body of knowledge surrounding this important topic.

During the review process, one of my personal mentors asked me what the next steps would be after publishing the field guide. I told her that I was going to create a website, a blog and a workbook to continue this work. She told me that we needed to create a million-mentor network. As audacious as that sounded at the time, it is entirely possible through the power of social media and the Internet.

Consider this your personal invitation to become part of that network by joining us at www.mentorintelligence.com. This site will serve as the hub to create that million-mentor community as well as to offer new insights, tools as perspectives as we continue our personal journeys to grow Mentor Intelligence™. Until then, thanks for taking this first step – it's always the hardest - and remember, a hand up is never more than one click away!

# Endorsements

Alan Landry has written an extraordinarily clear, easy to understand and insightful book that can literally change the way you live. This book provides a wonderful step-by-step approach and methodology to mentoring for people in the workplace, community or at home.

I believe we have untapped potential within to do great things in life. We all have potential that needs to be unleashed and developed to achieve results. Mentors can be key to this process. Mentors have played an important role in my life and I believe that I gained valuable insights into how to think more like a winner through engagement with a mentor.

In this book, Alan uses relevant stories and real life examples that will help the reader understand the vital importance of mentoring. One-on-one mentoring in the workplace or community can provide life strategies to change career paths enhance interactions with others and exceed expectations in many areas.

Everyone is designed with greatness inside and this book will provide you tools to reach purpose. Alan Landry's book is an excellent resource for everyone. Leaders and aspiring leaders should use this book as to become more influential and powerful as mentors.

Are you ready for a change in your life? Good! This book is for you. Alan Landry shows the heart of a mentor with a passion for excellence as he shares with the reader his life experiences and insights. As evidenced in this book, Alan is known across the nation as one of the best mentors around.
**Dr. Amanda Goodson**

Each chapter deserves an entire book. There are awesome nuggets of wisdom in those pages - and not just about mentoring - about life.
**Anonymous**

The day I received Al's request to write a testimonial to include in this wonderful book, I panicked. Not because I couldn't think of what to say, but because there are so many positive things I can say and the idea of trying to get them all on paper is frightening . . . so, I will do my best to crisply describe the Al I know.

Al's passion for learning and sharing knows no bounds. I have yet to meet another individual that cares so deeply about each person he meets. He regularly shares his failures so that all those coming up behind him don't make the same mistakes. This makes him an admired leader and most importantly, a trusted leader.

Al's book is a recap for those of us fortunate enough to personally know him; the road map provided herein works. I've watched the effects of Al's philosophies enable coworkers to accomplish personal goals previously thought unachievable. I've watched many, many early career employees grow exponentially just through the experience of having Al as a mentor, or through his organization, ELSWG.

Specifically, early career employees learn the business more effectively by "hearing the truth" about leadership decisions. Many times, early career (or even mid career) employees don't have the network or exposure to "connect the dots" regarding tough or controversial leadership choices. Al thoughtfully shared his perspectives and day-to-day experience and provided ELSWG mentees with guidance and learning that otherwise would have been unattainable. ELSWG meetings generated a sense of purpose for attendees and the natural outcome of this wonderful group was and is inspiration.

Although Al has moved on to the next chapter of his life, his legacy is alive and strong within the network of bright and amazing younger leaders imprinted with his meaningful insight and personal investment. Personally, knowing Al made me want to be better, period. It is one thing to be considered a great leader or a great person, but it is uncommon to be both. Having Al as the role model to care, lead, know, learn, and live made me want to be more than just a mentor; more than just a good boss; more than just a good mother. I hope you feel the same after reading this small excerpt of his amazing life's lessons.

**Rhonda Amstutz**

Al has a spirit that he cannot help but share, and his book is a great inspiration for any mentor, mentee, and anyone looking for more meaning in their life and work. I have been blessed by having Al as a mentor in my life; he brings a surreal level of passion with his holistic views on leadership. Take the time to reflect on his notes and tools not only as a mentor, but personally - and be amazed at how much clarity you can bring to your life.

**Tiffany Cremer**

In Al's "A Personal Leadership Ecosystem" section of "A Practical Guide to Mentoring", he touches on our Life's Legacy and asks "When you are gone, what will be left behind, and will it really matter?" This question is one that I highly resonate with and one that highlights my experience with Al Landry. I met Al at a diversity conference for the company that we worked for back in 2008. We were at a reception and he was describing a BBQ Lettuce Wrap recipe to a small group of people. I was instantly drawn in, as an aspiring foodie, but also and more so because I had never seen anyone in an aerospace and defense company speak so passionately about food in a setting like the one we were in. During that conversation we made an instant connection, and I quickly realized that this guy is not passionate about food only…rather, he is passionate about life. As time passed I realized he was not only passionate about his life, but had tremendous focus in injecting his enthusiasm into his sphere of influence in efforts to drive a culture that focuses on the things that matter. This could be seen in his many inspirational presentations given at college hiring events, employee resource group gatherings, leadership learning courses, and throughout the company during various cross functional assemblies. His dedication to mentoring individuals and groups, such as the Emerging Leaders Strategy Work Group (ELSWG), is also testament of his desire to influence a leadership culture he hoped would be weaved into our personal fabric. As I grow as a leader, I consistently feel that selflessness is one of the keys to making it all mean something. I am unsure that when I am gone if the company will remember me for the good products I delivered. What I am sure about is that when I am gone, I will be remembered by the people that I have touched. They will remember me in a good way or in a bad way. I focus every day making sure that it ends up being good, and in a way that positively shaped their journey and growth. I know that it will matter because I have met and got to know Al Landry as a mentor and friend, and I won't forget the passion and leadership that he inspires in me.

**Charles Everett**

As one of Alan's mentees, I reflect deeply about my career and life with his guidance and encouragement. I have created new mentorship relationship with mentees of my own with ease and confidence. Alan empowers his mentees with a unique ability to face their own obstacles and appreciate themselves and others while championing a true respect for differences. I highly recommend Alan's book for anyone interested in benefitting as both a mentor and mentee and learning best practices of engaging in these life-changing relationships.

**Susan Fant, Owner & Founder, Castle Sands LLC**
**Executive Director, Foresight Education & Research Network**

Climbing the corporate ladder is always an ambiguous race however, being in the defense industry as a young single Hispanic female, didn't make it so easy. Not that I thought I had the odds against me, that was other people (I think). The issue wasn't the climb, it was why and what I was climbing. Alan Landry answered my cold call to him and I made an appointment. I knew he was the man us young up-and-comers spoke to when they reached a perplexed moment in their career or life. He made himself available to those who just wanted to grow, learn or lead. I knew that was me and I told him just that. Who knows what he was thinking after that comment, but we met that same week.

When I walked into our meeting room, it literally was a war room. What I didn't know was that I was going to experience being in one. A war of the minds! We talked about goals, dreams, and it couldn't get more intentional that having a packet to follow and my Myers Briggs dissertation by the time our meeting was over. I left the room learning that my personal and professional life needs to be dealt with together, because they affect each other and I left wanting more.

I believe in having professional chemistry with the one that mentors you, it keeps the defenses down and the communication vibrant. Or, maybe that's when you meet with Al. He brings life to the table and challenges your goals and posses the right question so you can get to the right answer. Mentoring became a course of action and I new that I better start taking notes and doing my homework. I wanted to sharpen more than my professional skills, I wanted to make sure my mind and heart were aligned, so I can lead and serve professionally in hope of creating a foundation for others to build upon.

I was fortunate enough to be invited to join his ELSWG group where I was able to meet some of the most outstanding leaders in our corporation. Being invited and experiencing my first meeting immediately dissolved a myth I believed about leadership. Thinking it was exclusive and selected by others. I was wrong. Leadership is a choice that we make everyday in every situation. We are all people working towards a common goal of leadership regardless of rank, race, gender or monetary status. Understanding, what leadership means in our own world and how to respond with each other is what made the difference.

One of my life changing moments with Alan, was when I suddenly lost my uncle who had stood in the absence of my father and his loss shifted my perspective and challenged my character. Of course, I had to get up for work again and face the world. I picked up the phone and needed direction with work deadlines and grief in my heart. I shared my situation briefly and asked "How was I to deal with this all moreover, and lead a team?" Alan listened and gave me an assignment. I think my reassurance was not only that I had support, but in his availability and response. He knows his mentees, he takes that time and effort to push us to action and make a move. Even in the most difficult of times reminding us he is there. He taught me that being called to leadership, you are in the trenches, experiencing the awkward or difficult scenarios in the most inconvenient of times. He stayed late that day, listened and shared a life story so vulnerable and transparent that changed my perspective in the midst of my loss and in my life. Learning that when we lose we gain, and when we grieve, we are to listen and be present. Teaching that the balance in this life is one step and one piece at time. This critical time in my life not only enhanced my work, it helped heal my heart and family. It helped shape my perspective, so I can live out these values and positively infect the people in my world, activating my leadership in continuing these conversations and stories. Then watch the ripple effects. This unlocked fear and reiterated the value of relationships through vulnerability as you choose to lead.

Twenty-nine years ago I was born into a world and family that would determine some of the issues I chose to face. A man by the name of Alan Landry was brave enough to have the conversations about such things. Teaching to appreciate life lessons. When I respond to my experiences in my mind, heart or in the moment, I will not only grow and learn about myself, it would also create ripple effects that could change more that my own life. Overall, understanding that life is our most valuable teacher. One that instructs, takes, loves and gives primarily through and with each other (If we allow it to of course). I was so blessed to begin and continue this mentoring journey.

Alan Landry can be commended for his service to our country, the knowledge and experience he brings to a corporation or even the ability to speak and teach to and audience of many. Moreover, I know at the end of the day, this is the fruit of his everyday life through leadership and foundational values. His love is with his God and family and is always ready to teach, and be a life long learner in his world. Alan is creating a legacy that has laid a foundation for all people at any stage in life for generations to come. I am simply grateful to benchmark in creating one of my own and watch the ripple effects of leadership take its course.
**Kimmie Gross**

I met Colonel Al Landry when he was Raytheon's Director of Business Development for Land Combat Systems. I had just gotten out of the Air Force as a young Captain when I began working for the Land Combat team in the role of communications and public relations. Used to working for a single, easily identifiable commander during my time in the military, the complex organization chart I fell under left me with no less than four 'bosses.' Officially, Al was not one of them. Unofficially, he was the only one who mattered.

In a sea of smart people, I was drawn to Al's leadership and mentorship. He applied the principles of this book daily to a myriad of people, and I was one of them. Instead of drowning, I began to swim. Instead of 'getting by' I learned how my unique gifts could truly enhance the organization and contribute to the business effort. He offered his social capital, his decades of experience, and his honest feedback and support to me, and I am light years ahead of my counterparts for it.

Mentorship is a lost art, which is such a shame, because it can change lives. Tapping into someone's unique abilities benefits the mentor, mentee, and the organization in powerful ways. If you're a mentor now or plan to be in the future, pick up this book and learn how to unlock the potential in your people... their life won't be the only one that changes.
**Heather Healy**

Al Landry is, by far, one of the most upstanding gentlemen, friends, and mentors I have ever known. Al was there for me in the good times and the bad. He laughed with me, he cried with me, and above all he was candid and truthful. Al is a role model and truly "walks the talk". He created a group called ELSWG, Emerging Leaders Strategy Working Group, that took Raytheon by storm. It was a small, inclusive group where we all started the meeting with fears, insecurities, inadequacies and left heroes, warriors, shielded and prepared to take on the next challenge. Did Al leave a legacy behind? You bet he did. In fact we re-termed ELSWG, ALSWG; 'A' for Al. He taught

each and every one of us to "walk in faith", "be the change you want to make", that you can't be two difference people, one at home and one at work. Al taught me to integrate the two lives I was so desperately trying to keep separate. He helped me see that "leadership is a journey not a destination", that people can sense when you are not telling them something and therefore leadership requires transparency. Al demonstrated that one can lead from any chair. Al has truly provided a lasting impact in my life. The term "Life-Work" balance is an affectionate term ALSWG uses to keep us balanced. I can't put my finger on what it is about Al Landry, but his effect is unquestionable. He moves me, challenges me to be a better person, and holds me to an expectation that is achievable even when I can't see it in myself. Al is a true mentor for life.
**Mari Kulbacki**

Mentorship....what is the true definition? Merriam-Webster states it as someone who teaches or gives help and advice to a less experienced and often younger person. Another definition explains it as a personal developmental relationship in which a more experienced or more knowledgeable person helps to guide a less experienced or less knowledgeable person. However, true mentoring is more than just answering occasional questions or providing ad hoc help. It is about an ongoing relationship of learning, dialogue, and challenge.
To me these definitions are quite plain in the fact that they only express the abstract components of which mentorship is addressed. In a corporate environment these very types of relationships can feel exactly the same...abstract and void of emotion. They do not express the love, the heart, the passion and desire to build not only the personal relationship between the mentor and the mentee but the ongoing quest of positive change and character enhancement that is essential to personal growth.

When I was asked to write this testimonial for Mr. Alan Landry, an outstanding man of true character and dignity I truly did not know where to begin. I did not even know if I wanted to. It wasn't because I didn't respect him enough to write it, nor that he wasn't extremely deserving of it. But more the fact I didn't know if I respected myself enough, to provide the words that fit the feelings I had for the relationship we had developed in a very short time. I mean really...it was shocking that a man with such experience and stature would want a young black male who has not known him but a fraction of his life, write a testimonial for his first book? The answer was simple, but the action...not so.

My burning question in search for a mentor was where do I start? It was extremely important that I chose someone who shared some of my same feelings and struggles as a black male. To choose a black male who knew where I was at professionally and could provide perspective and help prescribe a formula to achieve balance and success. How do I choose the right mentor that fits my situation? I was a young strong minded black male unsure of his future and unaware of how to progress within Corporate America. Who do I choose? I mean, I knew of many capable black males within the corporation that were available for mentorship. Which one do I choose?

See, I am a thinker and will process a decision sometimes to my detriment. I have to say that this time around, my procrastination led to one of the best decisions I have ever made concerning my development and growth as a MAN.

Al's name was brought to my attention and I honestly could not tell, by the sounds of it, if he was a black male or not. It was kind of funny because I kept hearing about how passionate and energetic he was. How loud and funny he could be. How much he loved music and was always candid with his colleagues and mentees. I WAS SURE HE WAS A BLACK

MALE. I mean it did not seem real. This kind of leader...here in Corporate America...I thought I gotta get me some.

Then the fear and uncertainty presented itself. Not fear of meeting the man but the fear and uncertainty of being qualified enough to afford his attention. It's funny how retrospect can bring about the truth. Even in writing this, I cannot believe the thoughts of insecurity that would constantly consume my professional decisions as well as personal. They had a direct affect on my heart, which ultimately led to my inadequate performance.

Needless to say...my relationship with Al got off to a start I was not only unprepared for but also taken by surprise. He was unsuspectingly very open and honest about how our relationship needed to be in order for it to work. He mentioned that this relationship would only work if we were both engaged and if it wasn't a fit he would try to find an alternative for me. You see...the most important understanding I developed from my initial meetings with Al was that he would always be available and that as long as I was actively engaged in my own success he would never leave my side. That alone is a profound fundamental necessary in the cultivation of any relationship. To have the assurance someone is there to support you and trust despite your capabilities. Whether a child or a full grown adult, trust, loyalty and most importantly love are the beginning ingredients to success in relationships. Al not only possesses all these qualities but lives by them whole-heartedly.

I soon started to not be concerned about perceptions. Perceptions work twofold. The perceptions people have for you and the ones you hold for yourself. I used to perceive myself as less experienced without the necessary credentials to be truly successful. Therefore I felt people believed the same. Al has assisted in transitioning that train of thought into exactly the opposite. I have removed myself from first thinking negative and critical to believing in myself and expressing the qualities I naturally posses. Expression in the sense of vulnerability has been one of the main keys in my recent growth. I'm not sure Al understands that he has helped cultivate this without knowing through his own vulnerability. I have learned that vulnerability is not a weakness but one of the greatest emotions and tools for growth. It helps you understand exactly who you are, what you are capable of achieving and how much adversity you can truly handle. In doing so, leadership becomes subconscious as this very act unleashes others to do the same. For this alone I am truly grateful.

True leadership doesn't have a color or gender prerequisite. It shows no favor and bares its soul. For those initial thoughts I was absolutely wrong. I wasn't in quest of a black leader. I was searching for someone who understood me and was willing to come along for the ride. I was searching for a genuine leader who would listen and not fix my problems but provide perspective and share theirs. Al is more than just a mentor to me but a man willing to go the extra mile and show his love no matter what he received in return. He is reassurance and proof that God creates relationships to better the lives of everyone who is willing to take a chance and grow without any limitations. Thank you Al for everything I cannot express in this testimonial and for every way you will touch my life in the near and distant future. I am here for you and can truly say you are my BROTHA FOR LIFE!!!
May God continue to share your blessings!!!
**Kenny Neal**

Al Landry is a genuine leader in the best sense of the term. It's not just for his leadership technically, on programs, or in an office or on a field...the key part of that term is GENUINE. In his book, he focuses on the importance of building relationships as one of the keys of leadership. Al brings his genuine whole self and his whole heart to people as a leader and a human being; and he engages others where they are in their development. Al sets the example for building genuine relationships, taking the higher moral ground when relationships are in disarray, and building others through mentoring.

I have seen him change people's lives through concepts discussed in this book as well as allow himself to be changed by others. This work is not just for business leaders; it is for anyone who engages in relationships with others in life.
**Scotty Pignatella**

The minute I met Al Landry, I knew I had a lot to learn from him and I knew that he had a lot he wanted to share. Somehow Al managed to wrap up his life's lessons on mentoring, leadership and character into a powerful and succinct little package. Not only does this book help you become a better mentor, but the tools that are shared in this book are invaluable and provide a strategic way to look at your career and more importantly, your life. It also instills a sense of passion in you that makes you want to share your experiences with others so that you can make a difference in their lives - a "ripple", be it big or small.
**Veronica Garcia Quigley**

There are some people in life who radiate light, energy and love. Others are inexplicably drawn to them, you always leave encounters with them in a better frame of mind, and you find yourself wanting to find their internal source of goodness so that you might gain a little of it. These types of people are rare, and when you find one that has the time and desire to invest in you it can be life changing. Al has definitely been one of those people for me as well as many other young professionals. Right out of graduate school I jumped into the corporate environment and it was quite a culture shock. I grew up surrounded by family and friends on a large farm in a small town; Corporate America was unfamiliar and treacherous territory for me.

A couple of months in I knew I would need a trusted advisor to adapt and be successful in this new environment. I had never met Al, but someone who knew me well thought he would be a great fit for me. I sent him an email and though I was a complete stranger in a completely different part of the organization, he agreed to meet with me (and even gave me homework for our first meeting!).

Our first meeting was an experience I will never forget. For the first time in the professional world I felt completely comfortable and confident sharing my thoughts with a coworker, and even further a respected leader. Al generously gave me his time and energy for months after that, which completely shocked me once I learned how highly respected and sought after he was a leader and mentor. Al's ability to listen, ask the right questions, reserve judgment, and truly understand someone's personal character and values, enable him to be an extremely effective mentor.

In a few months he changed my perspective on my capabilities, my approach to my career, and what it means to bring my "whole self" to work. He repeatedly coached me through politics, bad leadership, personal issues, and anything else I brought to him. He was always authentic and candid, yet gentle and thoughtful with how he delivered feedback. I eventually transferred to a different location, but Al continues to be there for me when I need him. He helped me through one of the most difficult periods of my life and was a source of light and hope that I had nowhere else. He is that rare leader and trusted advisor that you can follow with your head, heart, and hands. I am so grateful that Al made his lasting mark on me so early in my career. His mentorship has been truly life changing.
**Courtney Schuster**

Alan's book provides the how to for successful mentorship. A unique type of relationship that helps an individual to be more than they ever thought was possible."
**Julie Copeland**
**CEO & President**
**Arbill Industries**

## About the Author

COL (RET) Alan Landry is an experienced strategist and leader in both government and industry with a unique passion for mentorship developed over nearly four decades. He leverages his insights in leadership and mentorship in a fresh, novel approach that can help any person be more effective in their own life as well as in serving others as a mentor. Alan has been married for the past 39 years to Paula Williams. They are the very proud parents of four children and ten grandchildren. Alan and Paula are currently enjoying life in Alpharetta, Georgia, where Alan manages his consulting company, ALtuitive Holdings, LLC.

## Contact Information

Alan enjoys hearing from anyone with insights and perspectives on leadership, mentorship, and diversity and inclusion. He can be reached anytime at 520-878-6074, or online at altuitveholdings@gmail.com

# Appendix A
# My "Letter To Me"

## My "Letter to Me"*

- **What would I tell myself 38 years ago?**
  - Life is about the **ripples** you will create in the **lives of people** you touch along the way
  - **Words** are powerful – choose them carefully, learn to **listen** to them and to hear them before you **speak** them
  - **Invest** in what is most important to you in everything. You will find that "what is most important" will change through the years. The one thing you can never make up is **time** whether in **assets** or **relationships**
  - **Coincidences** are really frames for **choices** you make within **intersections**; create them, enjoy them and marvel in their power to change lives
  - Everyone in life is either a **"giver"** or a **"taker"** – what is the **brand** you want to be remembered by? Then build your life around that brand
  - **Balance** is grace in action – seek it in all things, especially when it is most elusive
  - There is no real **perfection** in yourself or in others. Get over it (yourself). When you do, the **beauty of authentic diversity** will become clear
  - Learn to appreciate the real **value of what you do not know**
  - **Make it count** – every breath, every minute, every day – live a life of significance rather than self-importance. One is life giving, the other just intoxicating

*Title from a song by Brad Paisley, © EMI April Music, 2007

# Appendix B
# A Personal Leader Ecosystem

## A Personal Leadership Ecosystem

- **From what direction(s) do you lead?**
  - Up or down or lateral? Why? What is your motivation?
  - From the front or behind? Do you run to, or away from, the sound of "gunfire"?

- **How do you inform your decisions?**
  - Do you value what do you know more than what you don't know?
  - Do you know the difference? How?
  - How can you fill your life's "blind spots"

- **What do you reflect to your team?**
  - When they see you, do they see their qualities and potential or their shortfalls?
  - Do you really invest in diversity or in "sameness"? Do you run toward differences or away from them?
  - Do they see you, or themselves, in your image?
  - Do you "walk your talk"?

- **How do you wield your power as a leader?**
  - As a gift or an entitlement? What opens your heart, your mind and your soul?
  - With humility or arrogance? How can you tell?
  - Do you focus on good intent or good result? Why is that important?

- **Where do you point for successes? For failures?**
  - To yourself? To your team? To others?
  - Do you ever pass up an opportunity to showcase your team?
  - How important is credit to you (really)?

- **What do you leave in your wake?**
  - Do you lift others, elevate them or diminish them?
  - Have you inspired others to unseen possibilities or demoralize them with unrealized perfection?
  - Can you see more in others than they see in themselves, and provide opportunity for them?

- **What is the source of your personal funding?**
  - Can you answer the larger questions of life? Is your centering in self or something larger than self?
  - How do you "add to your account"?
  - What are your life debits and how do you pay them?

- **When you are gone, what will be left behind, and will it really matter?**
  - Is your life a life of personal achievement or a life of personal significance?
  - What does the balance in your personal life savings account say about your investments in others?

"To those whom much is given, much is expected."
— John F. Kennedy (The Uncommon Wisdom of JFK: A Portrait in His Own Words)

The most important tool in any leader's toolkit is personal example

146

## Appendix C
## Acronyms


BD: Business Development
CEO: Chief Executive Officer
COA: course of action
D/I: Diversity and Inclusion
DFK: Dreams For Kids
EC: Evaluation Criteria
ELSWG: Emerging Leader Strategy Work Group
GLBTA: Gays, Lesbians, Bisexual, Transgender and Allies
HR: Human Resources
JSWG: Junior Strategy Work Group
KAI: Kirton-Adaption Innovation Index
KIN: Kellogg Innovation Network
LGI: Large Group Interactive Dialogue
MBTI®: Myers-Briggs Type Indicator®
NATO: North Atlantic Treaty Organization
PAI: Personal Asset Inventory
SKAE: Skills, Knowledge, Attributes and Experience
SWOT: Strengths, Weaknesses, Opportunities, Threats
USMC: United States Marine Corps
VP: Vice President

CPSIA information can be obtained
at www.ICGtesting.com
Printed in the USA
LVHW081045121120
671515LV00030B/463